CW00495125

The Power of Authentic Leadership

Activating the 13 Keys to Achieving Prosperity Through Authenticity

by Jeff Davis
a.k.a. Mr. Mountaintop

http://www.jeffdspeaks.com

Published by eBookIt.com

ISBN-13: 978-1-4566-2861-1

Contents

Your Free Gift

As a way of saying thanks for your purchase and being willing to take the time to read this book, I'm offering you a free book: *Reach Your Mountaintop: 10 Keys to Finding the Hidden Opportunity in Your Setbacks, Flipping What You've Heard on Its Head, and Achieving Legendary Goals.* This book covers the ten core skills needed to transcend difficult setbacks, define your own version of success, and make enormous progress towards your vision. While it is motivational and inspirational, more than anything else it has practical strategies, ideas, and action-steps to get you to your next level.

Reach Your Mountaintop took three years to write and publish because I spent the time directly interviewing the world's top experts, and then featured their wisdom in the book. This book is still available for sale on Amazon and other retailers, but as one of my caring readers and supporters I genuinely want to reward you.

While the book you are reading is a deep dive into the power of authentic leadership, *Reach Your Mountaintop* offers a wider breadth of mindset, habits, and skills needed to revolutionize your life, lessons not taught in schools and most businesses. Everything you need to continue your journey to your personal Mountaintop, your own version of success, is included in **the free PDF that you'll receive when you email my executive assistant, Meg, at meg@jeffdspeaks.com.**

This free book is an excellent companion book to the one you are now reading, and will lead you to massive success, joy, and peace. Don't wait – email my executive assistant now and claim your free gift!

Introduction

Do you feel restricted by rules and red tape at work? Do invisible barriers stop you from reaching your full potential? Do you feel people are fake in their interactions with you?

I've worked for a Fortune 500 company and a startup; a moderately sized business and a 2-person company (me and one other person). At all of these companies, in one form or another, I was reprimanded for being myself. I don't mean that I was always literally yelled at. But I can genuinely and transparently say that whenever I challenged the status quo in even the slightest sense, I was discouraged from continuing with my initiatives. I was constantly told to "not rock the boat" and to "do as I was told." Even companies that said they encouraged innovative thinking in the interviews still frowned upon it when I followed through and actually did it in reality. The vast majority of companies and people say one thing and do another. It's the rare company and individual that will genuinely adhere to the values they say they follow.

For example, a Fortune 500 company I was a part of out of college (which I'll respectfully leave nameless) had a foolish policy in which all the employees in the whole department could not write anything off without their manager's approval. The write-offs involved balances owed by customers. I totally get needing the manager's approval for a big write-off, but we couldn't even write off one penny! Management had no trust in us, and it created an unhealthy culture. No judgment here, simply stating the facts: This was a huge failure on behalf of the management staff of this Fortune 500 company.

A huge flaw in corporate America – and for that matter, most companies – is when leaders do not empower their employees to properly do their jobs. Management and the leadership teams of many of these big companies talk a big game, but when push comes to shove they surround their employees with endless amounts of red tape. Please know that I'm not in any way insulting or putting down these companies. What I'm doing is putting forth, through decades of research and input from other experts, a better way. I'm here to say that through authentic leadership, employees who have some degree of autonomy are more effective at their jobs. In turn, companies as a whole become more productive and have a better work environment when employees are more engaged and feel more valued.

What does this have to do with activating the keys to achieving prosperity through authenticity? Everything. When employees of companies have red tape surrounding them, they feel restricted and unable to operate at full capacity. Specifically, employees feel like they can't be their true selves on the job because there's some sort of restriction on what they can and cannot do. And when you limit your employees' potential, they will leave your company. But when you give them an opportunity to prove themselves, you might be surprised by the quality and caliber of their work. When you give employees space to thrive professionally, their personal lives will benefit as well. Employees, business professionals, and all kinds of leaders need to be authentic because it will elevate their careers, expand their opportunities, and increase their job satisfaction. And regardless of your title, you *are* a leader.

The reason I shared this story from my experience at a Fortune 500 company is that when leaders become obsessed with the rules – and they forget about the people who are following those rules – they are limiting their ability to effectively influence others. Not only does their credibility suffer, but their authenticity suffers as well. Under strict rules that make no sense, people's productivity suffers, and they are not able to express their potential. The chapters in this book will help prevent a lack of productivity and engagement in businesses, groups, organizations, associations, schools, and anyplace where there are teams. Rules are not a bad thing *as long as they make sense*. The appropriate framework you've been looking for is in the chapters that follow.

This book will guide you through the steps necessary to achieve prosperity in all aspects of your life. In addition to showing you how to thrive in your career, it will also give you the tools necessary to succeed in your private life.

More than anything else, this book is an antidote to the way things have become. People, especially employees at companies (even those that are succeeding), have become so fake that it's become normal to be inauthentic. The truth is, it's not normal at all to be fake, and your true power lies in connecting with and expressing your authenticity. There is no substitute for being yourself. In a world where so many people are not *real* with themselves or others, I am going so far as to say that being authentic is the only true way to stand out and win at life. It's time to get rid of labels and embrace your inherent greatness.

This book features input from top experts, the most successful people on the planet: two Senators, a billionaire, New York Times bestselling authors, icons, luminaries, and extremely successful business owners. In addition to my own input and stories, I wanted to bring in the input from some of the most authentic leaders in the world to further validate the thesis of this book: You don't need to be anyone other than yourself to achieve prosperity and success. Rather than change who you are, you simply need to tap into and activate the brilliant essence that already exists at your core.

A successful Connecticut businesswoman named Piety Nadro, based in Trumbull, has specifically used the principles in this book to elevate her life to the next level. "Your work on authentic leadership not only transformed my life but also the lives of people I've recommended you to," she said to me. Rob Rowse, a businessman and accountant based in Maryland just outside of Frederick, said that the tips from this book allowed him to specifically tap into his core authenticity and maximize his prosperity. "Not only am I happier and more centered," Rob said, "but after reading this book I feel more successful than I ever have before because I'm tapping into and expressing my authenticity with the ideas I learned. This is the best book I've ever read in my entire life, and it enabled me to activate all aspects of my prosperity."

By the end of this book, you will no doubt be inspired to show your true self to your company and the world. In addition to being inspired, you will also walk away with practical insights and content you can use to activate true prosperity in your life – not only creating more wealth for yourself, but also more work/life balance, satisfaction, happiness, peace of mind, and meaning. The core theme is authentic leadership, and the experts I interviewed will also share with you a multitude of life tips and strategies to help you get to where you want to be. You'll know how to look at your daily activities from a higher perspective and utilize these timeless principles to have better relationships, make a real difference, increase your options, and enjoy life more. You won't just get prosperity; you'll *feel* prosperous from a mental, emotional, spiritual, and physical perspective.

When you are authentic, you will be comfortable and confident with yourself. You can use this skill when dealing with bullies and difficult people who are trying to get you to be someone you're not.

Let's now embark on this journey together. It's at times a scary process, but ultimately fun and rewarding. Most people will never face the truth of who they are, so the fact that you are willing to do this genuinely says a lot about you in the best possible way. It's an upward cycle of growth because the more you learn about yourself, the higher you'll rise, and on the other side of fear and uncertainty is peace and prosperity. By delving into the inner depths of your psyche, you'll be stepping into the life you truly want and deserve. It's yours for the taking right now as long as you read this book in its entirety and apply the lessons learned in your life.

Chapter 1: How to Deal With Bullies and Stay Authentic When People Are Cruel

"How people treat you is their karma; how you react is yours."
– Dr. Wayne Dyer

I was the quintessential late-bloomer, not hitting my growth spurt until my junior year of high school. I'm six feet tall now, but, for all of middle school and the first half of high school, I was one of the shortest kids in the entire school.

Additionally, some thought I had a slight lisp. I was extremely self-conscious about it after a few people unkindly pointed it out to me. During my senior year I wore Invisalign braces, which corrected my teeth and improved my speech mannerisms, but for many years I was embarrassed about my pronunciation of certain words.

I was frequently bullied for how short I was and the way I spoke. Since I had low self-esteem already, I felt like I was fundamentally flawed and unworthy as a person. It's safe to say high school was an extremely difficult time.

When I went to a small liberal arts school called McDaniel College down in Westminster, Maryland, I was ready to start over. I was especially looking forward to meeting new people and leaving the days of being bullied behind. That's when I met Tom (name changed to protect his privacy).

The Worst Bully I Ever Had to Face

Tom was on my college baseball team. He was the meanest, nastiest, cruelest bully I've ever had to face in my life.

Tom hated my guts, and to this day I don't know why. I'm an analytical and observant person, so here's my educated guess: One of my values is kindness, so when I meet people I am friendly. Perhaps Tom didn't think I was one of the cool kids because I was "too nice."

Tom hung around fellow bullies, people who enjoyed making fun of people. There was nothing Tom enjoyed more than disrespecting others and making them feel unworthy, it seemed; perhaps because it made him feel better about himself.

Tom didn't bully me for my height or for the way I spoke; he bullied me because of my general lack of confidence. I was afraid of him, and he knew it.

At one party, he told me to go hide in the closet. At another party, he made me feel so unwelcome and embarrassed that I left the party. At the gym once, he purposely bumped into me in an aggressive way and then walked away.

Why did I do nothing while he treated me like this? Two main reasons: One, no one ever taught me how to properly stand up for myself. I did not have the skills, tools, or know-how to assert myself. Two, in my senior year of high school I came incredibly close to committing suicide. There was still a part of me wondering if I belonged on this planet.

I had acne that wouldn't go away, and because I didn't like myself, I subconsciously thought maybe I deserved to be treated like garbage. Ridiculous, I know, but my self-esteem was low at that point in my life. Bullies like Tom prey on people with low self-esteem, and I was his prime target.

I stopped going to any baseball parties or social functions. I sat in my room by myself on Friday and Saturday nights. While my teammates were partying, I was letting my social anxiety get the best of me.

My anxiety ran sky-high when the thought of Tom crossed my mind. I was letting this one person dominate my life. I became depressed because I never would have expected bullying to continue into college. I wondered if things would ever get better.

The Silver Lining

After some dark and isolated nights—made easier thanks to phone calls with my awesome younger sister Annemarie—I realized I had to stop letting Tom ruin my college experience. I started to introduce myself to other people on the campus. I joined other groups and made all sorts of new friends.

I only saw Tom and the rest of my baseball teammates during a practice, game, or mandatory team function. Many of the other players on the team looked up to Tom as the leader of the pack, the tough guy they admired, so they weren't people I felt comfortable being around.

While I chose McDaniel College to continue my baseball career, I decided to stop spending time with people who didn't think highly of me whenever I could. I made many great friends at my college, and very few of them were on the baseball team.

I ended up having a great college experience because of this. If not for my experience with Tom, I may not have extended my social circle that far.

So I have two words for Tom: Thank you. Thank you for redirecting me toward kinder, more loving people. Thank you for giving me the motivation to introduce myself to new people instead of limiting myself to some silly clique.

Eventually, some of the other players on the team noticed how many people I knew at the school. A few them even said I was popular. I realized something profound then: When you are rejected by a person or group of people, life has given you an opportunity to expand your horizons, meet new people, and make new friends.

My senior year of college, with my confidence finally starting to rise again, I had the guts to go tailgate with my baseball teammates during a school football game. Tom punched me square in the face and then immediately left before I had a chance to say or do anything.

A week later, I saw him at the library. Rather than retaliate or seek revenge, I asked to have a discussion with him, and he agreed.

He told me he punched me because I was drinking his friend's beer—the beer that was supposedly for all the players on the baseball team, except me that is. I was the only one on the team harassed for this.

Tom went on to say that freshman year he didn't think I was one of the cool kids. He explained that he didn't hate me as a person, but he didn't agree with a lot of the things I did.

"Everyone has their own opinions," he said. I had no idea what he meant, as my freshman year of college I was always kind and respectful to others, but rather than inquire further into his inner world I kept the discussion brief. More than anything else, I was glad the feud was likely coming to an end.

I don't know what made Tom kinder than usual in this final conversation of ours, but as we made eye contact, he could see the big black eye he gave me. He didn't outright apologize to me, but he clearly felt sorry for what he did. His words and actions were conciliatory.

Perhaps he respected that I had just spent two semesters abroad, studying at McDaniel's satellite campus in Budapest, Hungary, as he did mention my travels in our discussion. He probably realized I'd made the most of my opportunities and had an enriching college experience, despite his continual and incessant disrespect.

To my surprise, he ended the conversation by shaking my hand. We then peacefully went our separate ways. By that point, he had quit the baseball team, and I no longer had to see him every day. He never bothered me again.

How to Move Beyond Bullying

Dealing with bullying is never easy or pleasant, but it comes with the territory of being human. Bullying happens not only on sports teams and in schools, but also in the workplace and other organizations. I hope these tips will help you deal with the cruel people in your life and come out on top.

Have Compassion

Having compassion for your bullies is extremely difficult to do in the moment, but it helps to remember that people who are hurting tend to hurt people.

Bullies want to make you think there is something wrong with you. The truth is, there is nothing wrong with you, and the bullies are the ones who are broken. Deep down inside they feel scared and unworthy, and they believe the way to build themselves up is to tear down someone else.

Have compassion and honestly feel bad for people like this. As I recently learned from my friend Evan Carmichael during a YouTube live discussion with him, this does not mean you must say out loud that you have compassion for them. It's something you can do in your mind, heart, and soul. Practicing compassion makes it easier to not take things personally, and to not react emotionally.

Don't Let Their Opinion Define Your Reality

Tom thought I wasn't worth hanging out with, but the truth is I have a lot to offer people. Despite Tom's opinion of me, I ended up making plenty of friends.

In what parts of your life are you letting cruel naysayers limit you? You are not defined by what other people think; you are defined by your actions and what you think of yourself.

Don't let a bully change the way you view yourself. The next time a bully says something to you that isn't true, pause. Then calmly say, *Oh, really?* Shrug your shoulders and move on with your day. The bully will most likely be neutralized. They are looking to get a reaction out of you and feed off your defensiveness. When you show them that their opinion means little to you, they will tend to leave you alone.

Meet New People

A bully is one person. There are lots of great people out there in the world for you to meet. Don't let one bad egg, or a few bad eggs, spoil the bunch.

If you are in school, join other groups that interest you. If you are in the workplace, attend networking events and other kinds of social outings outside of work each month. The person who will change your life in a positive way is one step beyond your biggest doubt. Don't be afraid to get outside your comfort zone because it will show you that the world is filled with awesome people.

Talk to a Close Friend or Family Member

When I was all alone on a Saturday night in my dorm room, isolated from my teammates, and before I met new people at my college, talking to my sister on the phone helped to remind me of all that was good about me and my life.

You are only alone if you choose to be alone. Reach out to a trusted friend or family member you feel comfortable with and vent your innermost thoughts and feelings to them. It feels good to have a listening ear, someone who reminds us of our value. Sometimes we get so caught up in our problems that we forget about the wonderful person we are.

Don't Cross the Line Just Because They Do

My sophomore year of college, while I was drunk, without thinking, I went to Tom's dorm room with a friend, knocked on the door, and went in. It was confrontational, but more than anything else it was an insecure "let's be friends" kind of thing.

My incoherence, coupled with the fact that he really didn't like me, made this a really bad and immature idea. By doing this, I opened up old wounds. His inexcusable actions were definitely on him, but it was not the right time, and I was not in the right state to talk to him. We didn't get into a fight that night, and he was actually pretty calm in the moment, but it gave him more incentive to bully me in the future since I'd invaded his private space.

Remember that just because someone else crosses the line doesn't mean you have to cross it as well. You're not responsible for what someone else does to you, but you are responsible for how you respond to it.

Assert Yourself Without Overreacting

When dealing with a bully who won't leave you alone, sometimes you need to assert yourself without overreacting. To respond in an even-keeled way, focus on asserting how you feel. Use "I" statements rather than "you" statements as much as you can.

When you accuse the bully, it will egg them on to keep going. But when you focus on how you feel, it will point out to the bully that they've crossed the line. Here are some examples. Try to do this during one-on-one conversations, but say it in the moment if necessary:

- I don't like the disrespect. Please stop.
- I feel frustrated that I'm not getting my space. I'm not getting any respect.
- I don't like how our conversations are always one-sided. I need to share my thoughts too.
- I don't deserve this. I deserve better.
- I'm not happy with this. The negativity is pointless. Stop it, or we're done.

These tactics did not work with Tom for many years, but they might work with a less extreme bully.

Send Them Love and Forgiveness

The late, great Susan Jeffers has an exercise I absolutely love. When you are alone, imagine the bully you are dealing with as a child. Surround them with light and love, and repeat in your mind, *I send them love, I send them love, I send them love.*

I was so afraid of Tom that he became a monster in my mind, dictating my actions around campus for a while. The truth is, he is a person just like the rest of us, and something went seriously wrong in his upbringing. You don't know what the bully has been through; they've become this way because they are hurting on the inside. Send them love and forgiveness.

Go to the Authorities When Needed

Be the bigger person, but only do so up to your limits. After Tom physically attacked me with a strong punch that left me with a bruised eye, I was at my limit. In one last attempt to end it, I peacefully confronted him face-to-face, and it worked.

I don't believe in retaliation or violence, so I stuck to my values even after he physically hurt me. With that said, if he attacked or threatened me even one more time, I would have gone to my coach as well as the campus authorities.

When a bully turns into a criminal, please do not ever be afraid to contact the authorities. The bully wants you to live in a prison of fear, but when they see you will not tolerate their actions, they will stop. The last resort before turning it over to the authorities is to tell them directly, "If this doesn't stop, I'm going to [person in position of authority]."

They may try to make you feel like less of a person for going to the authorities, but remember their opinion doesn't matter. All that matters is that you do what you need to do to find a solution.

Putting It All Together

Bullying is an international epidemic, and it needs to stop. But before the world comes to its senses, we're going to have to learn how to deal with difficult and nasty people.

The truth is we can't control how other people act, but we can control how we respond to them. By sending our bullies compassion, asserting ourselves, and choosing not to be defined by their opinions, we create a happy ending for ourselves.

The experience itself may be a nightmare, but you can peacefully move on with your life knowing you are a person of integrity and values.

You can move beyond the bullying you are experiencing, or have already experienced. You can find the silver lining and come out on top.

There is enormous power in being your authentic self, especially when dealing with particularly mean and hateful people like Tom. To move beyond the pain of your past and activate your prosperity, the first step is to forgive those who have hurt you and then use the neutral memory of the experience as fuel for the fire of your achievement.

Part of being your authentic self means sharing your most embarrassing moments with the purpose of helping others; if you're ready to share from a place of love.

Chapter 2: Do You Care How You Are Perceived?

"Train yourself to not be affected by the comments of haters and naysayers, knowing their comments don't apply to you."
– Evan Carmichael

My first conversation with my new friend Evan Carmichael happened in the late morning/early afternoon of January 12th, 2017. His vibe, energy, knowledge, and wisdom is simply incredible, and it was an honor to speak with him on one of his YouTube live broadcasts (I didn't even know you could do a YouTube live discussion until I met Evan).

Evan is a legendary YouTube creator, author, and entrepreneur, inspiring millions of people around the world to live their entrepreneurial dreams. He recently published a great book called *Your One Word: The Powerful Secret to Creating a Business and Life That Matter.*

Evan is one of the most sincere and authentic leaders I've ever met, so he's a perfect fit for this book and has great insights to share with us. He embodies authenticity at its finest.

What One Word Best Describes Your Core Values?

"In your interviews with successful people from around the world, I've noticed you are consistently authentic and yourself," I said to Evan. "What is the secret to being authentic in a world that is trying to get us to be like everyone else?"

"Know the one word that describes your core values," Evan said. "And model everything around that. I get brands who approach me all the time, offering me a lot of money to endorse them. I say no to a lot of them because they don't align with my one word. When you know your one word, you'll be able to place your values above the money."

"That's very impressive," I said. "Not a lot of people are able to say no to the money like that. You have integrity. Placing your values above money is profound."

The Importance of Self-Awareness

"Also, self-awareness is crucial," Evan said. "The moment you catch yourself doing something because you are worried about how you are being judged, you need to stop yourself and then do the very thing you were afraid of being judged for. I'm not going to let a stranger's opinion affect my actions. You catch yourself by being self-aware."

"I love that," I said. "Facing the fear directly and doing what you are afraid of being judged for is powerful."

"Yes," Evan said. "For example, one time I was listening to some music and dancing while at the mall. I could have cared how I was being perceived, but I didn't let that affect me."

This reminds me of an insight I picked up from Viktor Frankl in *Man's Search for Meaning*, one of my favorite books and considered by many to be one of the all-time greatest personal development books. Frankl talks about something called paradoxical intention, where you consciously do the exact thing you are uncomfortable doing. Evan mirrors this wisdom with his tips.

Yes, this is easier said than done. But when you muster up the courage to stop worrying about how other people perceive you, you'll thank yourself afterward and feel like a million bucks. Congratulations! You are now living a life that isn't dictated by external forces. In a world that's trying to get you to fit the mold and be like everyone else, that's a huge accomplishment.

Focus on Caring Less About How You Are Perceived

"This is excellent content," I said with a smile. "What are some tips and tactics you have for staying true to yourself and following your own inner compass even when other people are not agreeing with what you're doing?"

"There are two sides to this," Evan explained. "One side involves the haters and naysayers. With them, the key is to not care about what they think and say. Train yourself to not be affected by their comments, knowing that they don't apply to you. The other side is when people you work with don't like what you're doing. With them, the important thing is to find out why they don't like it.

"Someone you work with may think YouTube is stupid. You may love YouTube. Talk to that person and find out why they don't like YouTube."

What Evan is saying here is that when you seek to understand the people you interact with on a routine basis, you'll more easily see where they're coming from. Then you can objectively decide if you want to listen to their feedback and change your course of action, or stick to your original resolution because you know their opinion doesn't apply to your actions. Think in terms of solutions and constantly be forward-thinking by asking the question, *Where do we go from here?*

The theme of this book is for you to activate the power of being yourself by maximizing your strengths and living your life as an authentic leader. Evan is the perfect example of this for us to observe and learn from.

"I put zero – I mean literally zero – thought into how others perceive me," Evan said to me. "I don't show up needing the people who work for me to perceive me as some kind of hero or someone they look up to. It doesn't matter how others perceive you when you are being yourself."

Let's pause for a second because what Evan said here is so valuable, it's worth repeating. It doesn't matter how others perceive you when you are being yourself. If you are not living a life true to yourself, then you will be out of alignment with your core values. But when you are yourself, you don't need to concern yourself with what others are thinking about you because it literally doesn't matter.

Do you feel as liberated as I do right now? This is something I used to be horrible at. I'm much better at it now, with room for more growth. I, like many others, have a deep need to be respected and appreciated. There's nothing inherently wrong with this until it starts to define our self-worth. *Evan is helping us transcend this primal need by remembering that our self-worth is tied to how closely we are being ourselves, not how we are being evaluated by others.*

"I'm training a leader right now," Evan said to me, "and he's super concerned with how he's perceived by others. I'm doing my best to tell him that it doesn't matter how you are perceived by others. I don't care if others respect me or not. And guess what? I get lots of respect for that."

"You remind me of a quote from Dr. Wayne Dyer," I said to Evan. "He said, 'Those who get the most approval are the ones who need it the least.' You embody that truth to a tee."

Epic words from Evan here. Live by them, and you will soon find yourself being the epitome of an authentic leader like Evan is. This is Eckhart Tolle-level wisdom.

Jeff, You Stepped Up

Evan took it upon himself to compliment me.

"Jeff, you stepped up," Evan said. "A lot of authors want to do a private Skype chat with me, afraid of how they might be judged by others. But you came right onto this live YouTube discussion. It's awesome you did that. It's more exposure for you and shows you aren't afraid to put yourself out there".

"Thank you for saying that," I said. "It's a pleasure to be here. I also give you a lot of credit for showing up every single week, putting out awesome and inspiring content to the world."

Why am I pointing this out? Because Evan, by being himself, has exhibited a core aspect of leadership: encouraging others, complimenting them, and making them feel good about themselves. Evan has done way more live interviews than I have and easily could have kept the focus on himself. Instead, he used his social awareness to compliment me. Authentic leaders point out the strengths in others and make them feel good about themselves. It's alright to give others constructive feedback, but only after you've first complimented them and made them feel good about themselves.

Be Transparent and Vulnerable

"Do you find there's value in revealing your mistakes, flaws, and weaknesses to the world, with the specific purpose of helping others? What are your thoughts on that?" I asked Evan.

"Yes," Evan said. "We've all had struggles, and it's helpful to be transparent about them. I got divorced from my previous wife, and that was a tough time. But I got my 7-year-old son from that marriage, and I love him dearly."

Evan just hit a homerun with this comment, like he's been doing with everything else he's been saying. In my previous book, *Reach Your Mountaintop: 10 Keys to Finding the Hidden Opportunity in Your Setbacks, Flipping What You've Heard on Its Head, and Achieving Legendary Goals,* one of the main themes was that true leadership is about finding the silver lining in difficult situations. With this comment about his 7-year-old son, Evan embodies his leadership prowess as well as his maturity.

First, it took courage for Evan to reveal that he's been divorced. Second, notice how Evan wasn't negative about what happened. Yes, what he had to experience was unpleasant and challenging. But he was quick to point out how he now has his awesome son.

Being transparent and vulnerable means pointing out to others what went wrong in your life. From there, being an authentic leader means focusing on the good that came from the situation. Focusing on the good is not the same as disregarding the bad. It's important to acknowledge the bad, so you can process and fully feel what happened. Facing the bad also provides benefit to you and others. When you shift your focus to also sharing the silver lining, you are using negative situations from your past as springboards for others to learn from.

Internally Feeling Sorry for Others

"Your thoughts are beyond awesome," I said to Evan. "Let me ask you – there are people out there I've spoken to who apply all these insights we're saying. Yet, they still feel pushed around by the outer focus. Their friends doubt them. Few, if any, people believe in them. They are moving forward but struggling to fully break those chains. What advice do you have for them?"

"It's true that not everyone around you is going to believe in you," Evan said. "This even happens with family members. Here's my advice. Feel sorry for people like that. And that doesn't mean you need to literally say out loud to someone, *I feel sorry for you*. If you say it out loud, it will come across as a defense mechanism. What I'm saying here is to internally, on the inside, feel sorry for others.

"It's okay to go to a Thanksgiving dinner to spend time with your family and loved ones, even when you know not everyone there will be supportive of your goals, dreams, and initiatives. Let's hypothetically use Grandpa Joe as an example here. You may know ahead of time Grandpa Joe is going to go out of his way to be unsupportive of you because of the way he is and the way he chooses to be. Still, go to that Thanksgiving dinner. Enjoy the time with your loved ones. Here's what you need to remember and apply in your life: There's a difference between hearing what Grandpa Joe says at the dinner table and letting his words affect how you live your life."

This is unbelievably enlightening and one of the most powerful quotes I've ever heard in my entire life, and that's no exaggeration. There's a difference between hearing someone's input due to circumstance and letting it determine the choices and decisions you make. Here's the beautiful part of this process: You don't have to let the naysayers in your family deter you from your life's true course. Be respectful, internally have compassion for friends and family members who are putting you down, and then go about your life exactly as you were: being truly and authentically you. If you must be around a negative family member due to circumstance, be the bigger person and then make a conscious choice not to listen to their irrelevant words.

"Some people failed at turning their dreams into reality, or they never tried to achieve their dreams to begin with," Evan pointed out. "So, they attack and tear down anyone who is going after their dreams, afraid that others will do better in life than they did."

Evan reminded me of a former manager I had at a Fortune 500 company I used to work for in Maryland, right out of college (the same company I referred to in the introduction). I decided to leave the company after a year of being there to pursue opportunities that better suited my career interests. I was enormously grateful for my time there, but it was simply time for me to go. My boss was supportive, but my boss's boss, the Director, was the one who didn't like my decision. He was a big fan and "friend" of mine while I was unhappily living under his rules, but the moment I decided to go my own way in life, he suddenly became my worst critic. The Director not only severely criticized me for my decision, but made it a point to publicly humiliate me. Our department achieved our yearly goals, and we were all about to receive a monetary bonus. The Director deliberately took my name off the list so I would not receive the company bonus, even though I was still working there when the bonus was issued and had earned it as much as everyone else in the department.

Even though his words and actions hurt, I remained nonreactive and didn't take it personally. I didn't fight or push back at his antics; I let him be exactly as he was. I couldn't possibly have been more proud of myself, as my core flaw in high school and college was that I was constantly overreacting to people and turning their problems into my own. No judgment and no criticism here, merely a statement of fact: My boss's boss from the Fortune 500 company I worked at refused to empower others. He missed the boat! The best leaders empower others, giving them the autonomy needed to prove themselves.

Shortly after leaving, I emailed him a genuine thank you note, saying that I appreciated the time working for him; after all, we did have a good working relationship before the weird ending. I share this story to show there's enormous value in Evan's wisdom: Don't overreact to people who treat you poorly and you will win.

People who are attacking and tearing down others (trust me, I've encountered PLENTY of people like this, as I'm sure you have as well) are missing the point of life. We are all in this game called 'life' together, and we're here to help one another. Comparing yourself to others is pointless and a waste of energy. The best leaders are the ones who encourage others to go beyond their own accomplishments and surpass them. The best leaders are happy when other people do better than they are doing and they cheer on other people's success. The winners in life encourage others, and the losers in life tear down others. Which do you choose to be?

"Leaders create leaders in others," Evan said. "So many people out there are intent on stabbing people in the back to get ahead. This is not the way to be."

What Evan is saying here is that authentic leaders seek to bring out the best in people.

Combine Multiple Passions

"Last question," I said to Evan. "There are people out there who have a lot of competing interests. For example, they want to travel, but they also want to do other things. How do they get to know themselves better and decide what to do?"

"Your core genius lies in combining multiple activities," Evan said. "For example, if you only travel but have interests elsewhere, you are going to always wonder about what else you could have done. If you're only traveling and not pursuing those other interests, you're not going to make it big. It's going to be tough to be the best traveler in the world because there are tons of great travelers out there. But if you combine multiple interests and passions, finding the intersection, you'll have a better chance of standing out because you'll be operating from your core genius."

This ties into what authors and bloggers Jeff Goins and Chris Guillebeau will share with us later in the book. There is truth in the statement that great minds think alike: Evan's words of wisdom are the perfect setup for what we will hear from Jeff and Chris, and neither of them knew I'd also be featuring Evan in this book.

As far as getting to know yourself and your strengths, Evan looped back to the power of finding your one word, knowing your core values, and fully going after your passion. Read, reflect, talk to friends, spend time alone – do whatever you need to do to gain clarity on your values because they will be the guiding mechanism for making right decisions for the rest of your life. A lot of people know clarifying their values is important, but they don't actually do it. Do not be one of them.

Remember These Tips as You Continue Being Yourself

Before we leave this chapter, I'd like to leave you with two core themes from my discussion with Evan that will help you continuously live an authentic life amidst the constant twists and turns. The first sentence in each point is Evan's, and the remaining explanation is my own.

1. *Avoid negative people and step away from unsupportive networking groups.* I love this advice. A lot of the time our biggest problems come from the fact that we continuously put ourselves into situations with negative individuals. As Evan pointed out earlier, sometimes we are forced to deal with people like this. But a lot of the time, it's within our power to spend more time with individuals who uplift and encourage us. If you are in a group that isn't supporting you, step away from it. I recently stopped going to a networking group because of the negativity of some of the people in the group.
2. *It's a learning process.* The journey to fully being yourself, becoming an authentic leader, and living your purpose is an ongoing journey of ups and downs, trials and tribulations, setbacks and triumphs. Begin to view each experience as a learning situation instead of a failure, and you'll make progress more effectively.

Apply These Tips in Your Life

If you apply in your life the insights from this chapter alone, your life will be forever changed. With this chapter as your ultimate foundation, you are now ready to conquer the world. And you're going to love who we hear from next.

Chapter 3: Be Authentic While Making Difficult Decisions

"What I find really difficult is making career decisions. Normally it will take me two weeks, until the very last minute and I have to say yes or no. For a couple of weeks, I will tune everyone out who is giving me advice, so that I can make a clear decision on my own and it takes time."

– Paul Walker

Jared Kleinert is a superstar award-winning author of *2 Billion Under 20*, TED speaker, successful entrepreneur, and an overall awesome guy. I first met him after seeing him speak at the National Speakers Association Conference in Washington, DC, in July of 2015. We connected at the event and ate lunch together after he spoke. He also introduced me to several other successful speakers who became friends and valuable connections of mine. I resonated with Jared's energy. In November of 2016, we reconnected and had the pleasure of spending the day together in New York City.

What I love about Jared is that as successful as he is, he's down-to-earth and genuine. He didn't have the vibe or aura of "I'm better than you" even though his level of success is incredible. When we first met, I remember a number of people coming up to him and talking to him. He could have dismissed me as a nobody or told me he didn't have time to speak with me, but he invited me to lunch. On top of that, as I said above, he facilitated my introduction to some big names in the speaking industry. Awesome, right? I say this respectfully, but I've met a lot of people in my day – some who are part of the National Speakers

Association – who didn't have the common decency to treat me like an equal. Jared definitely wasn't one of them.

I've made it a point to only feature genuine and authentic people in this book. Here's the first big lesson I learned from Jared, and it came from him leading by example: *No matter how successful you become, stay humble and treat others with respect.* Too many people let success go to their head, in the sense that they then think they're above others. By all means, be confident, fully believe in yourself, think big, and act bigger. At the same time, please don't become so full of yourself that you forget to be decent to others. This is crucial to your ongoing success. I've met people who got big heads because of their success and started to treat other people like garbage – which ironically limited them achieving more success. (For more on what I'm referring to here, check out the second chapter of my book *Reach Your Mountaintop.*)

I had the honor of speaking with Jared on the phone to pick his mind about his success for this book. We also hung out in New York City for a day during the weekend and helped one another with the projects we have going on. Be sure to check out his book *3 Billion Under 30.*

Core Realizations on His Way to Success

"I've been an entrepreneur since I was 15- going on 16-years-old," Jared said. "I worked for companies in Silicon Valley doing unpaid internships."

Right off the bat, we see that Jared surrounds himself with world-class talent and people of high-level success. By taking the initiative, being proactive, and making a powerful internship opportunity happen at a young age, he exposed himself to opportunities that wouldn't have been there otherwise. This has been a powerful factor in his success.

"What really opened me up to a whole new world of connections was when I attended the Thiel Foundation conference and met influencers from around the world. When I left that conference, I started to really inspire others. I also encouraged others to join in the craziness of entrepreneurship."

"That's awesome," I said to Jared. "Surrounding myself with the right people was a huge turning point for me, so I'm definitely relating to you here. As this process was occurring and you became a man who inspired people all around the world, what are some of the key insights you had? Take me into your core realizations."

"I realized that my insights helped not only young people but also people in the corporate world and older generations as well," Jared said. "My book *2 Billion Under 20* has helped people of all different ages. I also realized it's important to understand where your life is coming from. What I mean by that is being aware of and understanding the biases people have. Take into consideration those biases when figuring out what you want to do. For example, once you are aware of the biases it will help you to choose options that give you more optionality in life, instead of diving into something you don't know for sure is what you want."

What Jared is saying here is that when you become aware of the biases people have based on their background and experience, *it increases your options.* Think of it like this: It's like being in a ballgame, and instead of going crazy trying to beat the other team, it's about increasing your awareness enough to realize that there are entire new stadiums and ballgames to enter into. Another great analogy is that of a landmine. There's nothing worse or scarier than walking through a mine field when you don't know where the landmines are. But when you know where they are, you can actively avoid them. That's what Jared is talking about. Being aware of what you don't want allows you to avoid potential missteps and more effectively get to your desired destination. It also allows you to take people's prejudices with a grain of salt, respectfully reminding yourself that their background may not apply to your life situation and goals.

"For example, if you are not sure whether or not you want to go to college," Jared said, "take a gap year instead of diving into something that may not be right for you. I like to emphasize the importance of increasing optionality. You can live anywhere in the world. As James Altucher says, live your life, not someone else's. It all comes down to how you make decisions. Are you going to listen to people who don't really know what they're talking about when it comes to the industry you want to join? Don't do that."

"That makes complete sense," I said to Jared. "You're a successful guy and very well-connected. How have you become authentic and what do you do to maintain such a large network?"

"Part of being authentic is having authentic interactions with people," Jared said. "Openly share your obstacles with others. As you build your network, it can be hard to manage all those connections. To balance that out, make sure you have meaningful and authentic relationships, interactions, and conversations. I also make sure to only bring certain people into my network. This may be perceived as inauthentic by some people, but there's a big difference between being a jerk versus being selective. You can be authentic while choosing to not connect further with certain people because they're not the right person for you.

"Treat people with respect, but choose to spend a lot of your time with people who lift you up. These are two different things."

I love what Jared is saying here, and I resonate with it. I always do my best to be respectful to others, even when they've given me reason not to be. On a rare occasion I might express some frustration if someone has really crossed the line and done something inappropriate, but as often as I reasonably can, I am kind because you never know what someone else is going through. Here's the thing: a lot of people get this confused and mixed up. They think that if you're kind to someone, it means you have to include them in everything you do. This is not the case. Make someone feel good about themselves and maintain cordial relations, but don't have a false sense of obligation that you *have* to include someone in your daily operations if they aren't a good fit for you. This took me a long time to learn, and I wish I would have learned it earlier on in my life.

"How do you maintain being humble while you are achieving at a high level?" I asked.

"I make sure to not treat people differently based on how they might fit into my relationship-building efforts," Jared said. "Someone I meet may not be the best fit for my network, and they may not be someone I desire to stay connected to over time, but I'm going to make certain I treat them as an equal and with respect. The last thing you want to be thought of is a jerk or someone who treats people badly."

"That's so beautifully said," I said. "A lot of people never learn or understand this lesson, and it limits their success. They think it's okay to treat people like garbage, but in doing so, they end up sabotaging themselves. It's definitely okay to be assertive and stand up for yourself when and where necessary, but someone shouldn't be a jerk just because they can be. And more often than not, people are jerks for no reason other than they enjoy being jerks."

"I agree," Jared said. "Looping back to what you asked me earlier in terms of being authentic, I also want to point out my style of relationship building. What I do is find common ground, opening the playing field up to the other person and meeting them where their interest is. I'm fully conscious of making sure I spend time with the right people. But I don't want to be a bad person, so I'm always respectful to others. This is a HUGE thing to remember when leading authentically."

Jared just touched on part of his core genius, and what he said is so powerful it's worth repeating: *Open up the playing field to the other person and meet them where their interest is.* Although Jared will not spend time with the wrong people, by showing genuine interest in others, he increases the likelihood that a genuine friendship and connection will occur.

We've now arrived at a crucial insight. Integrating this idea into your life will cause your prosperity to bloom:

Treat people as equals and be respectful to others, even if they aren't the best fit for your network. The last thing you want is to be thought of as a jerk or someone who treats people poorly.

Remember, you can't give away what you don't have, and what goes around comes around. If you give people judgment and negativity, that's what you'll get back. If you judge others, that's what you'll get back. This is not a feel-good motivational saying; it's a statement of fact. If you aren't sending love to others, it means you aren't a loving person. Let's follow Jared's example and implement his mature realization into our daily lives: How you treat others is an important part of your prosperity and success.

What is the Core to Leadership?

"Like everyone else I've been interviewing for this book, this is really valuable information," I said to Jared. "I know there are a lot of people out there who look up to you, and you're a leader. What are your thoughts on leadership and how it ties into achieving prosperity?"

"The more I can speak openly with people, the more people speak openly with me," Jared said. "You have to be willing to take feedback from others. It's not the easiest thing to hear, but the more objectively I can take feedback, the more objectively I can handle leadership. Getting feedback also helps me from a decision-making standpoint. It's a balance between subjecting yourself to the input from others and being emotionally intelligent enough to know when not to listen.

"Get to know the people who work for you. For example, I sometimes have to have a difficult conversation with a team member, asking for feedback on a blog post or one of my other publications. The feedback may be shit, but if you hear that feedback, it's very helpful."

This ties in perfectly to what we're going to hear from legendary blogger Jeff Goins in the next chapter, so stay tuned.

"Another thing on leadership I'd like to add," Jared said, "is being able to see down the road a little bit. As I write and publish my books, as well as speak, I think about where that's leading me and my business."

Here's the point: While leaders are busy focusing on the behavior necessary to take action today, they are simultaneously thinking about how what they're doing today ties into where they're going tomorrow. Leaders have *vision*. What vision do you have for your life?

How to Deal With the Craziness of Life

"What are some hacks you have to maintain your level of prosperity over time?" I asked. "What I love about your efforts is that you not only achieve a certain level, but you maintain it over time."

"It's important to really define WHY you do things," Jared said. "That'll keep you going over time. Also, understand yourself and how you make decisions. Anytime I feel like crap, or I feel down, I feel a lot better when I do some sort of gratitude expression. It might be looking at something uplifting on my phone or reminding myself of something I'm grateful for. I recently traveled from Cincinnati to New York, and I was absolutely exhausted from the trip. But I caught myself, and I took a moment to look up. I thought, *Wow, I'm in New York.* Taking everything in around me instead of getting caught up in my tiredness helped me to feel better. Also, smiling has a physical effect on your body. When you smile, it makes life less painful and more enjoyable."

"Those are great tips," I said. "I know you travel a lot. Is this for business, personal reasons, or both?"

"Both," Jared said. "I left NYC for a few months because I wanted to not see people. This was not for a negative reason, I just wanted to give myself some space to be creative without having the daily distractions. I did the same thing this past December as well. I'm a pretty social person, so a recent hack for me has been to take myself out of physical locations when I'm trying to do a launch or get work done. It's like when you are trying to lose weight, it's best to take the temptation of certain foods out of the house altogether. The same goes for your productivity.

"I've set up a consulting firm, and I take on multiple clients. Even with a lot going on, I keep delivering high-quality content, products, and services to entrepreneurs and aspiring business leaders of our generation. The vision—the goal—is to get our peers to act on their passions and solve society's biggest challenges while doing it capitalistically."

I love how Jared pointed out he makes money doing this. He's one of the most genuine guys you'll ever meet, and, at the same time, he also profits from doing what he loves. It's not one or the other. Both are true: Some people think that authenticity and wealth are mutually exclusive, but as we'll discuss more later in this chapter, this is not true.

"While I speak for higher and higher fees," Jared said, "I'm also interested in exponential ideas and actions, and in trying to do much bigger things. This might mean doing an online course, or something similar."

Things are going to be hectic on a daily basis. That's life. But don't forget the end game and where you're going. Look for ways to *exponentially* increase your success.

Making Difficult Decisions Leads to Exponential Success

The purpose of this book is for you to activate the keys to being authentic so that you will achieve prosperity, which includes mental, emotional, spiritual, financial, and physical health. In order to maintain your authenticity during difficult and trying times, you must have a framework for making difficult decisions. This is important because poor decision-making leads to stress and unhappiness. Please know that many of your decisions may turn out to be wrong decisions in the fullness of time, but with these tips from Jared, you will know how to make the best choices given the information you have in the present moment.

As we continued with our phone discussion, Jared opened up and told me more about his journey.

"I never went to college," Jared said. "Society would judge me as a bad decision-maker."

Yet Jared is the epitome of true success because he has defined and gone after his own version of success. He's started a successful company, Kleinert Ventures, where he consults with #1 New York Times bestselling authors, Fortune 500 companies, and VC-backed startups on product launches and overall marketing strategy. He's coauthored and published a book that's shelved all over the world and has sold thousands of copies. He now charges $10,000 as a keynote speaker to travel around the world and speak at conferences, colleges, and corporations.

"I have a network of friends, influencers, and mentors who deeply care about my success and well-being," Jared said, "and I've created incredible optionality for my future to start new businesses, create wealth, and invest in interesting life experiences."

Here's the point, and this is all shared for your benefit and for your enlightenment:

"It's because of the seemingly 'difficult' decisions I've made," Jared said, "that I'm able to achieve exponential success and impact, as opposed to making 'safer' choices that would actually be detrimental to my future, but seem 'by the book' to others around me."

Read that bold sentence above at least one more time, because it is without exaggeration one of the most powerful statements I've ever heard in my entire life. I WISH I WOULD HAVE HEARD THIS EARLIER (I get so passionate about this because no one ever shared with me these kinds of valuable insights when I needed them most, which motivates me to help as many other people as I can). But here's the silver lining and best part of this process: It's never too late to let go and start over, making the decision you've always wanted.

A Few Thoughts Before We Dive Further

As big and bold of an entrepreneur as Jared is, he does acknowledge and balance out doing work that matters with work that pays the bills. At the same time, there are ways to make money from doing what you love, and Jared is a great example of that.

"There are some cases where 'success' for you will require a more traditional path," Jared said, "like becoming a lawyer, doctor, or dentist. That being said, there are ways to accelerate your career and life even if traditional decisions are necessary to make.

"Also, I assume you want to deviate from the norm. If you are okay with the status quo, then, by all means, stay where you are. However, if you are reading this, there's a good chance you are growth-minded and want to continue developing new skills, advancing your career, and developing decision-making abilities."

If you've read this far, you're all-in. Let's go further.

Aligning Mission and Money

"There are people out there who have a passion or serious activity they take part in," I said to Jared, "but they don't make money from it. Is it feasible for someone to get paid doing their calling?"

"Yes," Jared said. "Let me use my publishing journey as an example. My mission is two-fold. I want to get as many people as possible to act on their passions in life, and then unite in solving the world's most pressing problems.

"My first book, *2 Billion Under 20*, had this mission, but because we went with a traditional publisher, all financial incentive to share the stories in my first book disappeared after the first few weeks of publication. The publishers owned the content, made money with each copy sold, and didn't care about our mission like we did. Their job is to sell books across hundreds, if not thousands, of titles each year, and so their big 'mission' is to generate sales regardless of the author whose books sell the most.

"By 'professionally self-publishing' *3 Billion Under 30*, I align our mission with money. I can apply industry-leading marketing strategy to the book's launch and sales over time because I control all aspects of the process. Every time I sell a book, I make money, and therefore I'll be indefinitely incentivized to share the stories of individuals who have invested their time and energy into helping me carry out my mission.

"For most people, however, this isn't the first decision that is considered, even though you could make the argument that it is the most important. In fact, traditional publishers are usually considered due to an author's lack of 'product' knowledge (how to make the book), ego (dreaming of hitting a credible bestsellers list), or because it is simply the standard path. All of these are bad ways to make important decisions.

"Here's a better way. Ask yourself, *What are my goals business-wise? Mission-wise?* It is possible to align purpose and profit once you are clear on your answers to the questions mentioned above. Elon Musk runs SpaceX to make humans multi-planetary as a way to avoid existential crises, and also to make money. TOMS Shoes helps those in need while also operating as a for-profit company.

"In both cases, and almost all others, where the purpose-profit alignment is clear, the companies actually make more money, have a better culture, and mean far more to their customers than if they solely operated to drive a mission or to make money.

"Simply put, I see this new publishing model as the best way to make this change in my business, and I have an obligation to myself and all those who have contributed to the *3 Billion Under 30* mission to put financial incentive behind our work as much as possible."

Let's stop and look at an important reflection point here because this point is subtle yet incredibly powerful: To authentically align mission and money, you must *improve your decision-making ability.* You must step away from the "normal" and "expected" decisions; instead think creatively and outside-the-box like Jared and other luminaries. Following a traditional decision-making process often leads to losses and failed ventures.

Incredibly enough, my publishing journey is remarkably similar to Jared's. I went through a traditional publisher for my first book and while it was a valuable experience and I don't regret doing it, the publisher kept all the profits from the print sales of the book. With my second book, I got a little smarter. I self-published and kept more of the profits from book sales. For the record, making money was NOT the main purpose of publishing the book. The main purpose of *Reach Your Mountaintop* was to spread an important message about how to get through dark and challenging times, find the silver lining in your life, and live your own version of success. With that said, here's what Jared and I are telling you: **There is a way to authentically make money while helping others, living your purpose, and doing what you love.**

For the longest time, I believed people making money to be inauthentic. This was a misperception on my part. Focus on *how* you are making money and *why* you are making money, seek non-traditional paths and options, and you'll find that there are more ways to make money with your business than you may have initially thought.

With decision-making being such a crucial part of authenticity, you must be asking right now, "Jeff and Jared – this is all great and makes sense. So HOW to do I make decisions?"

I'm glad you asked.

How to Make Difficult Decisions

"Whether or not you're an author or entrepreneur, hopefully our discussion up until this point will have opened your eyes to the level of thought needed to provide your own friends, customers, and individuals in your life with value, care, and engagement," Jared said.

The following is a checklist to follow as you make difficult decisions.

See Who Else Has Made Similar Decisions

"When I decided not to go to college, it was in part because many reputable thought leaders spoke out against its validity," Jared said. "The Thiel Fellowship, UnCollege, Enstitute, and other programs showed there was an alternative for some of our generation's outliers.

"I looked for alternate paths by seeking council from those who had made similar choices and succeeded, not opinions from those who'd never considered a different path and therefore had tradition (and their choice to abide by it) to protect.

"In my career, my family and mentors showed me that entrepreneurship would be the right path for me, especially creating a 'solopreneur' type consulting path. This path would allow me to work with high-level individuals and pay the bills in only 20% of my working time while investing the remaining 80% of my hours into longer-term projects like *2 Billion Under 20* and *3 Billion Under 30*. These long-term projects would take years to network, build, and ultimately develop into a sustainable and scalable business.

"Between reading *The 4-Hour Workweek*, attending some events from marketing legend Eben Pagan, and working for a VC-backed startup since sixteen, I soon realized that no one cares about your degree so long as you get the job done. There are ways to build networks, skills, and companies that don't require traditional paths or prerequisites.

"All of this I learned from studying the successes and mistakes of others before jumping into similar difficult-seeming decisions myself."

Seek Subject Matter Expertise

"In addition to studying those who made similar decisions, other information can be sought out to protect the downside of difficult decisions should you continue your pursuit of them upon further review," Jared said. "For me, this additional knowledge almost always comes in the form of mentorship or consulting with people who have deep knowledge on very specific questions or factors I'm still considering.

"You can see this in the consciousness of our marketing plan for the book launch. Not only did I study those who have made similar 'professional self-publishing' moves in the past like Tucker Max, James Altucher, Kamal Ravikant, Taylor Pearson, and others, but I also then sought out the specific experts for email marketing, or paid advertising, or design.

"With each new conversation comes the opportunity to solidify your stance on a pending decision, or change it because you are unsure that the bet you're making is worthwhile."

Lose Your Ego and Make Your Decision Scientifically

"Even after gaining all this knowledge on the industry and being in a position to reasonably bet on which decisions are best for you, our egos get in the way of us executing those difficult decisions," Jared said.

"For me, it means giving up the possibility of making a New York Times, Wall Street Journal, or USA Today best sellers list for at least the first half of 2017, if not forever, in order to pursue meaningful sales and collect customer data. Only sales registered through retailers and Amazon count for those lists, all of which have complicated algorithms for selecting who gets featured. And, while I'd love to be on those lists personally, it is more important for *3 Billion Under 30* to speak to as many potential readers as possible and be in a position to provide those people with as much value in the future as possible.

"Also, in order to finance the team I hired and the first print run for the book, I needed to raise a small amount of money from family and friends. My ego hated this idea because I've never asked for help financially in my adult life. From a numbers perspective, it was an intelligent business decision, because I only need to hit five percent of our sales goal for the book in order to pay everyone back."

Build Yourself a "Safety Net" by Increasing Optionality

"The good thing about making difficult decisions is that almost none of them are irreversible or everlasting," Jared said. "If you're stuck on what to decide regarding your education, career, or other situation involving a seemingly difficult decision (like whether or not to go with a traditional publisher as an author), always default to decisions that increase your optionality.

"By creating something like *3 Billion Under 30*, I'm building hundreds of deep relationships with influential individuals who would hire me in a heartbeat or otherwise refer me to new opportunities should I ever have issues with money or need a job.

"Instead of skipping school outright, I took two gap years. These were time periods where I tested other decisions but could have reverted back to being a student at any point in time.

"By becoming a solopreneur or consultant rather than being an employee to one company, you allow yourself the option to work with multiple companies and earn multiple contracts or income streams rather than relying on one organization to cut your paycheck.

"Launching a book in a way that doesn't rely on sales in a specific window of time, and financially incentivizes its author to sell copies indefinitely, provides optionality for how and when to sell product."

Straight to the Top

In order to land an opportunity speaking to the entire National Speakers Association in Washington, D.C. – the conference where we first met – Jared connected directly with the President of the NSA. He went straight to the top, and effectively connected with someone of power and influence. This strategy is a part of his core genius. You can bang your head against the wall for years on end trying to get through assistants whose job it is to block you. This insight alone could, without exaggeration, change your life (as it certainly changed mine).

I get that the head of a given organization may not have their email address or phone number available to the public, but if you do some digging, it may be easier to find than you initially thought. You can also ask someone you know and trust to refer you to the head of an organization, or someone near the top. Many people assume that the President or CEO of a company or organization is untouchable and out of reach, and that becomes their reality. But more often than not, these influential people are in fact reachable. Remember, they are people just like you and me.

One quick caveat and reminder: Don't let other people limit you. I was recently inside a company's building for an event. I was not there to specifically meet with the CEO, but I happened to notice he was available in his office. I walked in, introduced myself, and had a great conversation with him. This interaction led to some awesome things. After I left the office, despite it being a positive interaction, I received negative feedback from two employees of the company who felt I overstepped my bounds and was out of line to walk into the CEO's office.

Their negative reaction was more a reflection of their own biases, self-imposed rules, and limited viewpoints than it was the truth. Who cares what they think? I had the guts to authentically say hello to an influential business owner, and it led to wonderful things. Just because someone doesn't approve of your actions doesn't mean you are in the wrong.

"How are you able to reach so many people?" I asked Jared.

"I may only specifically connect with fifty to seventy-five people," Jared said. "But I'm strategic about my efforts. Those fifty or seventy-five people, through their followings and businesses, each influence millions of people. By influencing a small number of successful people, my efforts end up reaching millions of people."

This is the secret embedded within Jared's strategic thinking. It makes perfect sense. Think about it. If you go into a given company and want to make a difference in that company, you are much better off speaking with the CEO than with the employees. The CEO is the one who can endorse you, invest you, hire you, etc. (whatever your business goal is). This is absolutely nothing against the employees of the company, as those would make for good conversations as well, but what we're taking into account here is your business goal and the strategy necessary to most effectively achieve it. Why talk to the gatekeeper when you can go straight to the person who has the key to the castle?

Make a Decision

"Take these tips and turn them into an action plan of your own for authentically deciding upon a difficult decision in your life and executing that choice," Jared said. "The opposite of increasing optionality is crippling yourself through indecision. Every day you don't act, the opportunity to make a difficult decision wisely and effectively becomes more challenging and less rewarding."

Let's model after Jared and be strategic about our decisions. By following the process laid out here and stepping outside the norm, we will find ourselves achieving exponential success and fulfilling our true leadership potential. We will make an awesome difference in the world.

Chapter 4: Embrace Turning Points and Find Your Calling

"What if the thing you've always wanted
was actually right in front of you?"
– Jeff Goins

Jeff Goins's talent for writing and willingness to be himself has had a significant impact on my life, and now he'll touch yours as well if you haven't already come across him and his work. After exchanging a few emails over the years, I was lucky and blessed enough to connect with him over the phone, interviewing him for this book. Our conversation was a lot of fun, filled with enlightening gems of insights. Jeff is one of the top bloggers in the world for a reason – he's smart, genuine, and puts into action what he knows.

Be Authentic in a Way That Helps Others

Right off the bat, I asked Jeff about his take on the true meaning of authenticity.

"People throw the word 'authenticity' around as a euphemism for oversharing," Jeff said. "Some of my friends overshare and word vomit."

Jeff is all for being your authentic and vulnerable self – what he's saying here is to share yourself strategically and with purpose. Say what you truly mean and use your words carefully. Don't ever hold back and make sure to be who you truly are, but don't "word vomit" by randomly sharing whatever comes to your mind without thinking it through.

I went through some extreme challenges in high school and during my senior year, I emotionally hit absolute rock bottom. I was severely depressed and didn't know if I could go on with my life because I didn't have the tools needed to deal with the unexpected setbacks I was experiencing. When I'm doing keynote speeches to high schools, colleges, and certain kinds of conferences and associations, I share this story openly, honestly, and authentically. The point is I share it with a purpose after thinking through what I want to say and how I want to say it. There's nothing wrong with sharing your dark moments if you do it for the right reasons, in the right way, at the right time, and with the purpose of helping others. Make sure to think it through ahead of time.

"I've read a lot of your blog posts," I said. "One of my favorites is when you shared how you suck at life. You said in the post how you sometimes have a hard time staying on top of everything, and you let an email from one of your friends accidentally slip through the cracks. These are challenges many people, including myself, struggle with, and your authenticity was through the roof. I loved how open you were, and I really related to how you were feeling during those struggles. What are your thoughts on someone sharing their mistakes with the world, with the purpose of other people benefiting from the lessons learned?"

"Your ego tells you to hide and keep lying to yourself," Jeff said. "The key is to be honest with the world once that self-awareness comes. **Authenticity equals self-awareness plus sharing**. Share in a way that is helpful to other people. And always be interested in growing as a person."

Self-awareness truly is of paramount importance, as it not only allows you to recognize your shortcomings but also to share those shortcomings with others in the right way.

"I got beat up in high school for being short, pudgy, and not particularly athletic," Jeff said. "I couldn't bench one-hundred pounds. The more you share those kinds of things in ways people can trust, the more they will like you. If they like and trust you, you can lead them. They will be called to take action if what you said compels them enough.

"With my family, one of the best things I can do with my kids is to not lie to them. We don't pretend mommy and daddy are better than we really are. For example, if I yelled at my kids, I will tell them *I shouldn't have yelled at you. I'm really sorry.* This is much better than making it seem like the rules don't apply to you."

A lot of people speak down to their kids, making it seem like their kids are not their equal. Jeff's genius and authentic persona stem from his ability to be his true self with his family, kids, and everyone else he encounters in life. Jeff is a great role model and example for us all. **Being authentic is not about being perfect. It's about admitting when we're wrong and owning up to our mistakes.**

This is incredibly powerful and a great way to end this section. If you are feeling uneasy, don't view it as a negative – view it as a signpost, pointing you back to your true self:

- If you are feeling uneasy about a choice or decision, it may be time to reconsider the choice or decision and make a change if necessary.

- If you are feeling uneasy about being in a relationship, it may mean the relationship is not right for you – or, at the very least, it is time to confront your partner about what you are feeling uneasy about.
- If you are feeling generally uneasy about your day-to-day life, it may mean you are not managing your time well and making the most of each day. It also may mean you are not living your life according to your own values and ethical standards. Further, it may mean you are living someone else's life and not your own life. Is it time for a career change? Is it time to move to a new geographical location? Is it time to start meeting new people? When you use uneasiness to your benefit, you use it as the motivating force to make real, sustained, and long-lasting change in your life.

Instead of fearing your uneasiness, use it as a signpost to lead yourself to bigger and better things. And as amazing as all of that was, this is only the tip of the iceberg of what Jeff is offering us. Let's go deeper.

Choose to See Through Fake People

"My wife and I sometimes invite people over for dinner," Jeff said. "My wife told me once, after a dinner we had, how a guy we had over wasn't genuine. My wife said to me, *He's a jerk!* My wife explained how he was overconfident and egotistical. Overconfidence is a form of insecurity, and I can see it. I pick up on when people are like that. People can be fake."

I love Jeff's input here, as I can't stand fake people. I'm not perfect, but I always do my best to be as authentic and real as possible. My friends often tell me that I am the most real person they know. Leadership is about living your message, so I say this to point out that I'm actively applying everything we're discussing throughout the book with these experts.

An example of how I actively eliminated fake friends from my life is I permanently deleted my Facebook account. I then created a new Facebook account where I consciously became Facebook friends with authentic people. I do sometimes accept friend requests from people I haven't met in-person, but only if their Facebook profile is legitimate and they are someone I actually want to be connected to. When you are around fake people, both in real life and in the social media world, overconfidence and egotism become the norm.

Here's one of the main messages of this book: What has become normal in society is *not* normal. It's *not* normal to be fake. It's *not* normal to put on a false front and be someone you are not, out of fear or one of the many other reasons people feel the need to not truly be themselves. I say this respectfully: There are countless people on this planet who are fake. They surround themselves with fake people and then call their inauthenticity "normal." That's why Jeff's input is so refreshing, and our conversation was both fun and rewarding. I resonate with him in the innermost depths of who I am as a human being. This content has value to you when you apply it in your life. When you see through fake people and then choose to steer clear of them, you give yourself space to be who you really are. It also gives you an opportunity to get around people who are better suited for you. Leaders like Jeff see through fake people.

Seeing through fake people is a skill and habit that can be developed over time through practice. This is something I used to be bad at, and I'm much better at it now. But I'm staying humble and wary because the moment you think you're free of fake people, you get stabbed in the back. People also love to use you for your money. This is NOT being cynical, as there are a lot of good people in this world. It's simply being aware of the possibility of inauthenticity in others so you can more easily navigate around it.

Jeff's Big Turning Point

"You're very successful and one of the top bloggers in the world," I said. "Was there a specific turning point for you?"

"When I was going through school, I was insecure and unsure of myself," Jeff said. "I was bullied a lot. At that age, I was SO impressionable. People will say stuff about you, and if you choose to believe that, it can become true. When you're insecure, it's easy to let someone else's opinion become your own."

I was also very insecure when I was younger, so I'm connecting with Jeff here big-time.

"There was this really popular guy in my high school," Jeff said. "He played sports, got good grades, got the girls, he had it all. My freshman year, this guy died at the age of 15 of a heart attack. I was at a small rural school with three-hundred people, and the most untouchable kid in the school randomly died.

"It shook everyone up, including me. When this popular kid died, it made me realize how fragile life is, and that **it doesn't matter if you are cool or not cool.**"

This ties into what Evan Carmichael was telling us earlier about how it doesn't matter how you're perceived by others. I've always tended to care too much about how people perceive me, so Evan and Jeff are helping me tremendously. I hope you're getting as much out of these words as I am.

"After the most popular kid in my school died, I went from being shy to being outgoing," Jeff continued. "I started to go bowling with people, initiating and masterminding the details behind bowling outings. I made meetups happen with people, and I reached out. Three or four people would call me and ask what we're doing this weekend. One night, five people called me. I became the leader and people were looking to me for their plans."

I have a similar story in that I also used to be incredibly shy. After someone who I thought to be my friend told me in an unkind way I didn't talk to anyone, I reinvented myself and ended up becoming one of the most popular kids in my middle school. Popularity doesn't matter, but **the moral of the story is that you can use frustrating, challenging, and/or tragic moments as springboards to reinvent yourself and become the person you were meant to be.**

One of the keys to Jeff's turnaround in school is that he started to reach out and initiate things. You can't wait for things to happen – you must make them happen. Shyness is a mask that hides your true self. When Jeff and I became more outgoing, we stayed true to the core of who we were while deciding to talk to more people. Reinventing yourself involves implementing different behaviors and actions, but it doesn't change the core of who you are. Instead, reinventing yourself is a creative way to step into your true nature.

"I always wanted to be the extrovert," Jeff said, "but I was judged as a chubby, red-haired kid, and I let that become my reality. When the popular kid died, I said to myself *Screw this, I'm going to be whoever I want to be*."

Jeff just hit on an incredibly important point, deceptively simple yet incredibly powerful: Being an authentic leader starts with a firm, inner decision. It's mind over matter. Your turning point can come at any moment and at any time if you choose for it to be so. There's no need to wait any longer to change for the better. Why not make your turning point now?

Rewire Yourself With a Firm Inner Decision

To give you an example from my own life, let me provide a few more details from what I mentioned a few paragraphs ago about myself. I'm sharing this to help you with your own process. My supposed friend in Middle School, who I shared many classes with and hung out with outside of school, didn't invite me to one of his parties. He invited many people I knew, and I felt disappointed that he didn't feel the need to invite me.

In a moment of courage, I asked him why he didn't invite me.

"You don't talk to anyone," my fake friend said to me. "So there was no point in inviting you."

As a shy and sensitive kid with very few friends at that time, I was devastated. I went home and balled my eyes out to my dad, and he was supportive. That evening, while in my room, I made a firm, inner decision to become outgoing. The process of forcing myself out of my shy ways was long and arduous, with a lot of mistakes and awkward practice along the way, but I slowly became more outgoing over time. Although no one ever taught me how to properly socialize, I taught myself. I realized being outgoing is a learnable skill.

The point is changing your life doesn't necessarily have to come down to writing down lots of different goals, joining a ten-step program, or following a predetermined course of action. (For the record, there's absolutely nothing wrong with any of those options if they work for you.) Changing your life often comes down to a firm inner decision – a promise to yourself – that you resolutely stand by. Of course, there will always be ups and downs, progress and setbacks, but when your desire to change comes from the deepest part of who you are, you can literally shift the patterns and outcomes of your daily life.

I've been studying neuroscience and psychology for more than two decades, and I've interviewed many of the top minds in the field. The most exciting discovery from this research and experience is that you can rewire your brain through repeated actions. You can rewire the way you think, act, and behave through practice. This is not motivation. This is science.

What one new action will you take tomorrow to start rewiring yourself? And what behavior will you continue to enact on a daily basis over time?

What You Hear Isn't Necessarily True

Our phone conversation on a roll now, Jeff continued sharing with me his excellent wisdom and advice.

"We live in this age where everyone says to follow your passion," Jeff said. "I don't think they are particularly helpful."

Some people will tell you to jump off a cliff and grow wings on the way down. Jeff and I both don't agree with this approach. Let's take a test group of one million people. One or two out of those million people may be able to succeed in their venture by blindly jumping into it. But the rest of the people may crash. We tend to only hear about the success stories, not the failures. We hear from the few who make it, people who then scream from the mountaintops that the way to succeed is to jump off the cliff. Society tends to worship people like this.

Jeff and I are advocating for a more practical approach. There's nothing wrong with following your passion, but the zeitgeist gets us into trouble when it tells us to go after our dreams without ever showing us *how* to properly do it. If you are working a full-time job and wanting to become an entrepreneur, why not wait to replace your full-time income with your side passion before leaving your job? If you hate your job, then transition to a job that's a better fit for you. There's no need to jump off the cliff and put undue stress on yourself, just because you hear about someone's one-in-a-million, unlikely, success story. There's absolutely no need to compare yourself to that person. That's their journey, and this is yours.

Please don't misunderstand: I'm all for dreaming and thinking big. I'm all for doing the improbable. In fact, I live for that kind of stuff. I love proving people wrong and succeeding faster than anyone would have ever expected. And that's what you are and will continue to do. All I'm saying is to balance your big dreams with what you can realistically do in this present moment. In my own evolution as a person, I've found that success is more than just dreaming big dreams, although that is a great place to start. Success is about *doing.* It's about taking action and moving the needle forward each day. When I stopped getting endlessly caught up in the fantasy of the perfect tomorrow and started to embrace the reality of today, the irony is that's when I started to make real progress on my dreams.

When I left jobs to go after my entrepreneurial dreams *before ever having made money as an entrepreneur,* I fell flat on my face. This happened to me twice. I left well-paying jobs to go after this elusive dream of the good life of the entrepreneur, only to find that in reality, I had no idea what it really took to succeed as an entrepreneur. But when I approached the process from a more practical standpoint, that's (ironically) when my business started to take off.

Here's the point: Don't be fooled by society's obsession with *following your passion.* Instead, use the following process from Jeff to discover your purpose and your why. Then use that as a bridge to finding a career that's meaningful, and gradually make progress over time. This may not make for a good movie script, but it's the reality you must hold to if you want to most effectively embrace your authenticity and achieve prosperity.

Jeff's Three-step Process for Self-discovery

"Step one, figure out who you really are," Jeff said. "The only way to do that is to look inwardly. Ask yourself: *Who am I really?* Do some soul searching. Years of counseling and relationships have taught me that people do change, and the understanding of who you are grows and evolves."

Jeff explained to me that some people are rigidly caught up in who they are and how they act, in the sense that they feel like they will never change. This is a limiting belief: Both my friend Jeff and I have seen plenty of people change, including ourselves.

"Step two," Jeff continued, "is to get feedback from trusted sources. We really struggle with this in the western civilized world. We don't do a good job of inviting friends, mentors, bosses, and peers to say what they see in us. In one light, yes, people will tell you to do this or that, and it may not be relevant to you. But in another light, you won't find your true self alone. It happens in community when others see something in us."

This reminds me of Dananjaya Hettiarachchi's World Championship-winning speech *I See Something*, in which he shares how he became great because of what other people saw in him. I featured Dananjaya in my previous book, *Reach Your Mountaintop: 10 Keys to Finding the Hidden Opportunity in Your Setbacks, Flipping What You've Heard on Its Head, and Achieving Legendary Goals.*

"Derek Sivers says something that I absolutely love: *What's obvious to you is amazing to others*," Jeff said. "I wouldn't be where I am today without the friends and mentors I surround myself with. I was just doing an interview, and someone asked me the way I approach writing. It happens by engaging the community."

Jeff went on to explain that even as we actively seek feedback from others, it's not always easy.

"Some people are going to say things like *Who are you to try that? Don't do that!*" Jeff said. "Some people want you to stay in a box. So, this is a complicated and complex process."

What Jeff is saying here is, it's up to each one of us what we choose to apply in our lives. You have the final say when it comes to what you apply in your life. It's also crucial to surround yourself with the right people – people who care about you and at the same time will be honest with you.

"Step three is to meditate or pray," Jeff said. "Whichever works for you."

This is the perfect third step to self-discovery because it is through meditation and prayer that we can access our intuition and go with the decision that feels best to us. When we connect with the truth of our inner selves through silence, the noise of the outer world fades away.

One of the keys to achieving prosperity through authenticity is to live your life. If you don't have enough content to share with others, it may not mean you lack creativity. It may simply be an indicator that you need to put yourself out there more and really live your life.

Finding Your Calling

"Parker Palmer wrote a powerful book called *A Hidden Wholeness: The Journey Toward an Undivided Life*," Jeff said. "What it comes down to, is having integrity and being a whole person. This doesn't mean you are always going to be good and honorable, but it does mean you are who you say you are. When you are not true to yourself, you lose your integrity and disintegrate. Disintegration means you are falling apart on the inside. Being disintegrated from who you are will cause uneasiness.

"Palmer talks about the inner teacher. There's this resonance that occurs when you are doing what you love.

When someone points out to you, *That's it, keep doing that,* you know you've found your calling."

I love how Jeff also provides meaningful and authentic examples.

"An example is parenting my son," Jeff said. "When I see my son light up, I know I'm being a good dad. We know intuitively when we are doing something that feels true to ourselves. Your calling is that place where your deepest joy meets the world's deepest needs. You may have hobbies that don't meet the demands of the world. The sweet spot is that intersection, yet so many people are trying to find themselves by themselves."

It's a good idea to take time for yourself to figure out who you are. *Don't stop there.* This is where Jeff is saying some people get stuck. Instead of staying by yourself, go into the community and figure out where your talents intersect with the needs and wants of the world. "Nothing beats talking with someone face to face," Jeff said.

"Once a quarter, I text ten friends," Jeff said. "I send emails to former co-workers and old friends."

Jeff proactively engages with the people around him because he wants feedback and he wants to make sure what he's doing is relevant to others. This takes a lot of courage to do, and Jeff is leading the way.

"When I get in an argument with someone I'm close to, I sometimes tell them *This is who I am,*" Jeff said. "But the truth is my temperament is a choice."

Jeff, like the rest of us, has ongoing ups and downs, trials and tribulations. But through self-reflection and seeking outside help, he becomes aware of his areas for improvement.

"Sometimes people are doing what they want in a selfish and immature way," Jeff said. "That's why being true to yourself and finding your calling has two parts. One, ask yourself *Who am I?* Do that soul work and tap into your interests, passions, and things you love. Two, get that feedback. You cannot become self-aware alone. We find our true selves where self-awareness and community intersect."

Doing One Thing Versus Having an Overarching Focus

"To sum up what we've covered so far," Jeff said, "get people to give you honest feedback on the areas you might be missing. Also, listen to your inner teacher. When you do these two things, you will have a deeper appreciation for who you really are, as opposed to going off to the monastery."

What does Jeff mean by "as opposed to going off to the monastery"? He means rather than secluding yourself from others, society, and the world, seek to integrate these lessons into your daily life. There are parts of ourselves that want to be alone, and there are other parts of ourselves that enjoy being with others. Your most authentic self is where those two come together. To activate your authenticity, you must find the balance that works for you in finding community while also making time for yourself.

This may sound a little contradictory at times, but give yourself space to play with two opposing ideas in your head at the same time. Enfolded within spending time with others is the need to be alone. And at the end of alone time is the desire to be with others. *Both* are true. Jeff's advice is solving a problem I've had for a while: reconciling my introverted nature of needing alone time with my outgoing nature of enjoying socializing and going to networking events. There is value in having multiple sides to your psyche, and when these sides are merged together, your truest self will emerge.

Bestselling author Neale Donald Walsch agrees wholeheartedly with what we're discussing. I asked him on Twitter if ultimate truth can be realized in this moment, or if there is more to realize based on the foundational truth we now know. He responded with one powerful, enlightening word: *Both*. Sometimes you must hold contradictory ideas in your head at the same time. There are usually degrees of truth to both sides of a discussion or argument. The goal with this chapter, and the book as a whole, is to integrate seemingly contradictory sides of your psyche and find the authentic wholeness that is innately yours.

"What are your thoughts on doing one thing versus having an overarching focus?" I asked Jeff.

"The goal is not to be a Jack-of-all-trades," Jeff said, "but a master of some. It can be very risky to just do one thing, like an investor putting all stocks into one portfolio. The portfolio life is about diversifying yourself without spreading yourself too thin. Yes, pick one thing you really want to do, but typically when you master one thing, it leads to other opportunities."

Did you follow that? Jeff is *not* discouraging you from having that one thing you focus on like a laser. He's pointing out that in the process of having your one thing, more things will emerge – the need to master new skills, the opportunity to meet new people, etc. – and that's where you must delicately and strategically expand your horizons.

Jeff also pointed out to me that it's not important to fit in as much as it's important to focus on your strengths and excel at the things you are good at. In fact, a big part of Jeff's success was to focus on what *he* wanted to do, often not listening to the things other people said he should be doing. If what you are doing is to please others and not a reflection of your true self, it may be time to change. If your "one thing" isn't you, then do something else!

To be clear: This is not encouraging you to constantly jump from one thing to the next. It's getting you to implement a mindset that allows you to try different things, accounting for the benefit of widening your perspective while having a general focus. It doesn't mean you will try to do everything, but it also doesn't mean you have to only ever focus on one thing.

"A great example is Michelangelo and Da Vinci," Jeff said. "Michelangelo was all-in on sculpting. Then Da Vinci said to him, *Hey, painting is better*. They made a bet and Michelangelo lost, so Michelangelo picked up painting. The Pope heard Michelangelo was now painting and that led to Michelangelo becoming an architect. Michelangelo was essentially an entrepreneur.

"As was the case with Michelangelo, one thing leads to another thing, which leads to another thing. When this happens, you learn a couple complementary skills. Using myself as an example, my first and main skill is writing. My second skill is business and entrepreneurship, which is about making money. And my third skill is marketing. By creating value and then selling those things, I get the money I need to give myself more time to work and create.

"You are looking for one really focused skill, and then some complementary skills that benefit that main skill. One opportunity tends to beget another. You don't have to chase every single opportunity, BUT it is advantageous to combine a couple of skills in a unique way. This is what makes you marketable.

"Robert Greene, in his book *Mastery*, talks about mastering your craft and how the future belongs to people who take different skills and combine them in interesting ways. The company Apple really hit its stride when they introduced two different groups to one another: engineers and artists, people who love to make really functional things and people who love to use those functional things."

Create Daily Habits

"One of my favorite blog posts of yours was how you talked about the best year of your life happening when you stopped setting goals," I said to Jeff. "Do you think there is any value in having goals, or is there a better way to go about getting what we want while helping others?"

"I love achieving things," Jeff said, "and I do enjoy planning. But the best year of my life was not about a plan. At the same time, it wasn't just letting things happen either. It was about *habits*, doing what I could do right now to set into motion things that can continue without me. That was the year I went from working at a nonprofit job with a salary, to becoming a dad, starting a business, publishing two books, quitting my job, my wife quitting her job, and now chasing my dream. This was not the plan and this was not what I thought would happen."

"Would you say habits are the secret to your greatness?" I asked Jeff, smiling through the phone.

"Yes," Jeff said. "Creating daily habits. It's not about having these big, audacious goals. It's about doing the hard things now and the easy things later."

"That's very well said, Jeff," I said. "Right on the money. People have asked me how I've written several books. I told them it wasn't about conquering the whole mountain in a day. The key to success is taking it one bit, one day, one step at a time. It's alright to have a long-term goal, but it can't be something you do someday. Someday is an undetermined point in the future, which often turns into never. Your dream has to be something you work on today. What are your parting shots, my friend?"

"Do a quarterly review of your life," Jeff said. "I have a very formal process I go through. I ask feedback from trusted sources, connecting with good friends at least one day of the week. Some people are busier than others, so do what works for you regarding the exact timeframe, but I suggest taking inventory at least once a quarter. Ask yourself, *What did these last three months look like and what am I learning about myself?* Most people never do this.

"I just connected with my mentor, a twenty-five-million-dollar CEO of one of the top companies in the world. I asked him what he wishes he had more of when he was starting out. He said he wishes he got coaches and mentors to give him feedback much, much earlier."

You just got direct input and wisdom from one of the top bloggers in the world, and one of the greatest writers in human history. Take what most resonates with you from his remarkable insights and run with them. If you apply these tips into your life, you will achieve prosperity through authenticity and reap a lifetime of success.

I'll leave you with another life-changing quote from Jeff Goins, to show you what he's really made of: "It's not about ego for me. It's about helping people."

Now go be the authentic leader you were meant to be.

Chapter 5: Do You Always Hang Out With Your Neighbors?

"If you don't design your own life plan, chances are you'll fall into someone else's plan. And guess what they have planned for you? Not much."

– Jim Rohn

I got connected to Pete Kohlasch through my good friend Mike Shelah. Mike was featured in my previous book, *Reach Your Mountaintop: 10 Keys to Finding the Hidden Opportunity in Your Setbacks, Flipping What You've Heard on Its Head, and Achieving Legendary Goals*. Pete is an entrepreneur, certified high-performance coach, life strategist, and one heck of a guy. You're going to love his insights as much as I do.

We met at The Ginger Man, a cozy restaurant in Greenwich, Connecticut. Our conversation was epic and insightful. One of the keys to being an authentic leader and becoming prosperous on your own terms is to consciously design your life. Pete will show us how.

Choose to Live by Design Instead of Living by Default

"If surrounding ourselves with the right people is so important, then why do so many individuals continue hanging around people who are bad for them?" I asked.

"You can't have relationships by default," Pete said. "But most people automatically associate with their neighbors, people they work with, and family friends. If you want to achieve great things you have to be deliberate with your choices and relationships."

"That really resonates with me," I said to Pete. "Some people are going to help you, but there are a lot of people out there who will hinder you and hold you back. A lot of the times we hang around certain people simply because they're the people we've always hung around."

"Absolutely," Pete said. "If you want to make a million dollars, surround yourself with millionaires. If you want to go and work in the third world as a volunteer, then surround yourself with third world volunteers and workers."

"Love it," I said. "Things picked up for me in my speaking career once I got away from the naysayers and around other coaches, authors, speakers, business owners, entrepreneurs, marketers, philanthropists, and humanitarians."

"Yes," Pete said. "The thing to understand is that some will hold you back unconsciously, without even knowing it. For example, parents may have good intentions and love you, but not know what is best for you. That's why it's crucial to consciously make your own choices and decide who you spend your time with."

It's not like people are consciously trying to hold you back or hurt you. Yes, there is the occasional critic, but most of the time people stop you unconsciously based on their own limiting beliefs and thought patterns. Make it a point to surround yourself with successful people. Reach out to a couple big players in your industry each month. The possibilities expand when you get around *and stay around* the right people.

I'm always authentic to the best of my ability, but I become especially transparent when I'm around good-natured, confident, and intelligent people like Pete. So I decided to open up and share a challenge of mine.

"There's this friend," I said, "who I love to death. We've been good friends our whole lives. But whenever I'm around him, as much as I don't like to admit it, bad and dysfunctional things happen. I don't want to blame him for anything, but he's seriously the only friend of mine who this happens with, and it happens consistently. With most people, I wouldn't have a problem ending the relationship, but since we've been friends for so long and been through so much together, I find myself continually hanging out with him anyways."

"I understand what you're saying," Pete said. "Here's my food for thought: *The relationship was at its peak when the dysfunction was at its highest.*"

"That just struck a chord with me, and in a very deep way," I said. "Never were we closer to one another than the nights when we were doing things we shouldn't have been doing."

Here's the point: Be wary of people you've known for a long time who are in your life by default. The hardest weeds to pull are the ones that run deepest. Be selective of the new people you meet, but also be aware of the people already in your life who are bringing you down.

Create for yourself what Pete calls a RAP: Relationship Action Plan. Take an honest look at the people in your life and make an action plan to make changes when and where necessary.

Creativity is a Learnable Skill

Our conversation transitioned back to business, and we talked about how people tap into their creative genius.

"We're not born creative," Pete said. "It's about reading, developing, and spending time creating. That's how you become creative."

This is an incredibly powerful insight: Creativity can be developed and cultivated through practice. The same is true for leadership. Leaders are not born – they are trained and developed.

When it comes to authenticity, it can also be developed. As we discussed in the last chapter some people in the world are fake and aren't going to be a good example of integrity; you have to consciously choose integrity for yourself. This comes through practice. You may make mistakes along the way, but give yourself credit for making progress and make course corrections along the way. Treat every experience as a growth opportunity, and reflect in a journal to write down lessons learned.

Consciously Become a Better Version of Yourself

"It's all about becoming a better version of yourself," Pete said. "I love helping people win by showing them how to create a personal infrastructure. Once people know why they are where they are and where they want to go, I help them create the plan to move forward. This will skyrocket their productivity. After that, I focus on helping my clients with their physiology, psychology, and sense of connection."

Here is Pete's personal accelerator blueprint formula. The first word in each point is Pete's, and the remaining thoughts and explanations are my own:

1. **Awareness**. Use meditation, reflection, introspection, solitude, talking with a family member or friend, or any other technique that

works for you to raise your level of awareness. You can't improve your life if you aren't aware of the problem to begin with.

2. **Clarity**. Most people aren't clear about what they want and where they're going. Bring your target, your end goal and result, into focus.
3. **Strategic Activity** (bridging the gap from where you are to where you want to be and skyrocketing your productivity). Are you taking action in a thoughtful and purposeful way? Are you thinking through your daily activities and staying focused?
4. **Physiology**. Are you eating healthy? Are you monitoring your energy levels? Are you taking care of yourself and getting enough rest each night?
5. **Psychology**. Feed your mind with positive inspiration. Read great books, watch educational and inspiring YouTube videos, and monitor your thought processes. Affirm to yourself that you are a wonderful person – because you are.
6. **Connection**. As we heard from author and blogger Jeff Goins earlier, genius and creativity happen best in a community. Are you staying connected to the friends you want in your life? Are you steering clear of fake people? Are you maintaining a sense of connection to a higher power?

These six pillars are encompassed by what Pete calls a winning culture. It's an ongoing and continuous process, and you must keep growing, reflecting, and improving.

"I love *The Miracle Morning* by Hal Elrod," Pete continued. "My version of the miracle morning is taking a good five and a half hours to reflect and prepare myself for the day ahead. I also take time to engage in ideation, where

I think of different ideas I can implement in my business to better serve others."

"That's excellent," I said to Pete with a smile. "Your habits are awesome. You also have a really easygoing and peaceful way about you that I admire."

"Thank you," Pete said. "I'm always looking to improve myself so I can continue to help others. Here's my definition of the winning mindset: **identifying a purposeful pursuit; building the confidence and courage to pursue; consciously working into your best; facing and embracing the adversity that is inevitable in pursuit of your best; demonstrating the resilience to overcome; and producing a result you're proud to put your name to.**"

"You're brilliant Pete. I mean that sincerely," I said. "You're very creative, and I love how you think of all this stuff."

"Thank you," Pete said with a smile. "This all came from years of study. I spent a good six years reading and studying everything I possibly could. Then I spent a good 13 months creating my own material, via masterminds, webinars, coaching programs, and stuff like that. *Then* I went and did a program to become officially certified."

"It was a fantastic move to create your own program first," I said to Pete. "You really worked hard to create your own life."

"Exactly," Pete said. "The certification program I did supported what I already created. Too many entrepreneurs jump to become certified in someone else's program, but if you create your own program first, you'll be ahead of the game."

Provide As Much Value to the Marketplace As You Possibly Can

"I'm loving everything you're saying here," I said to Pete. "To play Devil's advocate for a moment, I know of all different kinds of entrepreneurs and business owners. Some of them make a strong impact, but their cash flow isn't as strong. Why do you think that is?"

"One of my favorite quotes of all-time is by Jim Rohn," Pete said. "He said, *You get paid by bringing value to the marketplace.*"

I nodded, jotting down Pete's words.

"If someone isn't creating the wealth they desire and deserve," Pete explained, "one of two things is happening. One, they have an inflated sense of their own value. Or two, their business development process is off. Or both could be true, or some kind of mixture of the two."

"That makes sense," I said. "A lot of times people bring the value, it's just a matter of tweaking and improving their business development process. Or it might mean having to study up to become more of an expert in their field. Do you mind me asking some of your major sources of income?"

"Sure," Pete said. "I do masterminds by helping people create a winning mindset; I have a Personal Accelerator Blueprint course designed to provide people the strategic plan and prowess to achieve what they want out of life; I do one-on-one coaching; and I also do team training built around establishing a winning culture."

The Secret to Success: Build a Personal Infrastructure Through the Cycle of Growth

"Want the secret to success?" Pete said enthusiastically. "Commit to engage in thorough preparation. From there, build, sustain, and maintain the courage to continuously perform. Assess your progress along the way through reflection and feedback, and commit to lifelong improvement. If you do that, you'll be well on your way to having a personal infrastructure, something most people go their whole lives without."

Prepare –> Perform –> Assess –> Improve –> Prepare…

"That's Mountaintop-level advice, my friend," I said.

This may sound straightforward, and it is, but you would simply not believe how many people don't apply this.

"A lot of people know this, but they don't put it into action," Pete said. "If you make it a point to apply this process in your life, you'll become the best version of yourself."

Don't Listen to the Naysayers

"There were a lot of people who told me I wouldn't be able to do this," Pete said. "There will always be a lot of people who tell you that you can't do something while you are on your way to success. As a twenty-eight-year-old coach, some people had limiting beliefs around what I was doing. But I kept on showing up and adding value. I proved myself, and people really started responding. People started to come to me looking for coaching, knowing I provided practical and valuable processes and solutions.

"Who I am is a coach who speaks. I've always just wanted to help people to *win*. As an athlete my whole life, I've used my success as a high school athlete to springboard into a life of achievement and helping others. To become a better version of yourself, my advice is to get a coach to challenge you to do that. The common denominator of successful football players, CEOs, singers, and Olympians is they all have coaches to help them get to the top."

Be your own coach. Use the material from this chapter to make improvements in different areas of your life. And as you continue growing, consider hiring a coach. I suggest you hire Pete or a coach of similar caliber. There's no hidden agenda here, so please be sure to do what's best for you; you don't have to hire a coach if you don't want to. All I'm saying is that Pete really is *that* good and he's earned my personal recommendation. I don't recommend a lot of people, but Pete is the real deal.

Creating Confidence: Feelings Come Last

Let's end this chapter with another one of Pete's epic diagrams on how to create confidence. The majority of people in the world have this backwards, so this formula alone will revolutionize your life when properly applied. Here it is, straight from Pete's hand:

Planning/Strategy/Preparation –> Produce (productivity)
–> Self-Confidence –> Self-Esteem –> Feel

Similar to what we were discussing earlier you start with preparation, which includes planning and strategizing. Once you have a plan, you will know what you need to do to be productive, and you'll be able to effectively take action. As you are putting yourself out there and taking action, you'll feel more self-confidence. As a natural byproduct of confidence, you'll have higher and healthier levels of self-esteem. *Then* the feelings will come.

This is genius. Most people – and I say this respectfully, having made the mistake myself – wait for feelings to come before they act. But as we just learned from Pete, the feelings don't come until *after* you act. If you are doubting yourself and feeling insecure, as we all do at times, *do* something that makes you feel confident. Notice that the doing (productivity) comes before the feeling. This was so important to touch on before we leave this chapter because as you are making changes in your life, the confidence won't fully come until after you are producing.

Confidence doesn't come from sitting around in your room all day thinking about how to be confident. It comes from putting yourself out there and adjusting as you go along. This is where the personal infrastructure and creating confidence comes together. The same goes for prosperity. You can only assess and improve after you've performed and prepared; accordingly, you can only feel great about yourself after you've built up your levels of self-confidence and self-esteem. And the self-confidence comes from productivity, which stems from effective strategizing.

Your next practical step is to sit down and strategize. *Think*. How do you want your day, week, and month to unfold? Where do you see yourself three months from now? What are some ways you can start taking action? This does not mean you'll get lost in strategizing, but rather it means you'll create an effective starting point to create lasting success.

"Can't wait to share this with others, this is remarkably valuable content," I said. "Pete, it's been an honor to talk with you today, thank you for your time."

"My pleasure," Pete said. "I look forward to getting together again."

Chapter 6: Break Free of the Expectations of Others

"You don't have to live your life the way other people expect you to."
– Chris Guillebeau

As we continue on our journey of activating the keys to prosperity through authenticity, one of the most important steps is to align our actions with what we value. One of the biggest challenges is that so few people practice what they preach. So *many* people say one thing and do another. It's become normal to make false promises and let people down. This is, in fact, not normal at all, and when people don't act out of integrity, it not only reveals their true colors but also limits their future success.

One of the most authentic and genuine people I've ever connected with is Chris Guillebeau. A New York Times bestselling author, speaker, entrepreneur, and world traveler (he's been to every country in the world, which is remarkable), Chris mirrors the wisdom of the other experts featured in this book: Being your most authentic self often means stepping away from the beaten path and from what's normal. Being authentic means going your own way.

Being authentic means revealing your true self to the world. And in doing so, you will attract the right people into your life. Being authentic looks good on paper, but is hard to put into practice. The goal of this book is not to pay lip service to the "idea" of being who you really are. *The goal is for you to actually, in reality, take off the mask and show your true self to the world.*

In the first chapter of my previous book, *Reach Your Mountaintop: 10 Keys to Finding the Hidden Opportunity in Your Setbacks, Flipping What You've Heard on Its Head, and Achieving Legendary Goals*, I shared the story of how I almost committed suicide in high school because of the unexpected setbacks I experienced. I've also shared this with tens of thousands of high school and college students in keynotes across the United States and the world. Here's the thing: Some people resonate with the story. And for the people it's meant to help, it helps them tremendously. At the same time, some people don't resonate it. Some kids look at me like I'm weird and don't accept me for who I am.

I fully realize suicide prevention is an uncomfortable topic, but in order to prevent more people from committing suicide in the future, it needs to be discussed and addressed. Too often, people tend to shy away from discussing the topics that matter most.

In order to reach the people I'm meant to reach, I put up with the haters, naysayers, and critics by not letting them get to me. The same applies to you.

Being authentic can be (and often is) fun, but it isn't always that way. Sometimes it's hard to be authentic. Sometimes it's the last thing you'll want to do. It's important to be who you really are even when it hurts because if you start compromising on the little things, you'll eventually start compromising on the big things. Bite the bullet and be yourself even when you don't feel like it, and you'll find yourself living a life of true leadership, courage, and difference-making.

We Choose What We Value

I had a chance to connect with Chris Guillebeau in several email exchanges, and his wisdom and insights are legendary, to say the least.

"We choose what we value, either consciously or unconsciously," Chris said. "Many people, young and old, have no problem happily spending their money and even going into debt for luxuries each week. I've chosen to focus my own spending priorities on meaningful experiences."

There are four types of important questions to ask yourself when aligning your life with your values. The questions are from Chris, and the thoughts that follow each question are my own.

1. **Am I satisfied with my work? Does it meet my needs and fulfill my desires?** We all have to pay the bills. We all have to grind. But you need to really examine your life and find out if you are settling. Be honest with yourself. Are you making daily efforts to create a better life for yourself? Are you looking into career alternatives? Are you thinking outside the box and considering various options? There are countless possibilities – this is not a motivational feel-good saying, but rather a real, practical fact. My Master's degree is in finance, but I ended up transitioning into digital marketing. You can make a transition as well, even if others think you can't.
2. **Think back to the times you have left your home country. What did you learn on those trips? Do you think you have more to learn?** These questions are awesome because they not only get you to keep things in perspective, but they also

remind you that there is always more to learn. Stay humble. Learn more about your career field and see if there are more aspects to it you may enjoy doing. Learn about new interests and stay fresh.

3. **If you could go anywhere in the world, where would that be?** Chris is an avid traveler, like myself. If you enjoy traveling as much as we do, great. If not, don't worry – this question applies to you as well. Are you spontaneous in your daily life? Are you creating new adventures? You don't need to travel to the other side of the world to do this. It could mean checking out a new local restaurant, hiking a local mountain, or even walking around town and saying hello to new people. Being spiritually prosperous means keeping life interesting. Be independent and never be afraid to do anything alone.
4. **What are your financial priorities?** Take a long, hard look at where you spend money. Are you living in your own apartment and getting killed by your rent payment? Consider moving in with roommates, your significant other, or back home with your parents if you are younger than 30 and have a good relationship with them. Are you tired of having to answer to a landlord? Sell your belongings, find someone else to finish out your lease, and go travel the world (that's what I did with the last apartment I lived in, and I'm better off for having done it). Yes, you sometimes need to make tradeoffs, but there are also more options and possibilities than you may have initially

thought when you really sit down and think about it.

You Don't Need a Niche

Now that we've discussed clarifying your values and evaluating your priorities let's take a look at why you don't need a niche.

"I've never had a demographic," Chris said. "I've had a psychographic of people interested in fun stuff."

The perfect example of this is Chris's annual World Domination Summit, attended by thousands of people. Over the last five years, more than ten thousand people have attended.

"It's a strength to not have a niche," Chris said. "It's a strength, not a weakness. For my summit, I knew I wanted it to be special, so I had to pick something that was deliberately broad. I had to because I knew I had to do a lot of different things to be satisfied, so that's why it was all about non-conformity. I did this for my own fulfillment, my own motivation, and also to serve the community – to be able to truly serve them."

When Chris said this, I got really excited. I've had a lot of conversations with people who say that you absolutely need a niche. From my perspective and experience, you don't need a niche. Here's where some people may misunderstand me, and where I can hopefully clarify what I mean in this chapter: They assume that I'm advocating for them to become a generalist. This is not what I'm advocating at all. **Continue to focus on your core areas of knowledge, but don't be afraid to branch out into additional areas of expertise.** I would never, ever encourage someone to speak, write, or talk about a topic they don't know anything about. But if you have expertise, experience, and/or knowledge in a given area, why stay away from it just because it's outside of one particular niche? Some experts will tell you to only focus on one niche, but that doesn't make sense to Chris and me. Make sure to only step into topic areas you have experience with and knowledge about, but don't be afraid to have more than one niche. Don't take my word for it, listen to what successful author Chris Guillebeau says.

Chris started with travel blogging, but even then he didn't focus on a particular demographic. As he mentioned earlier, he simply wanted to connect with people who enjoyed doing fun stuff – and his content and insights could help them do exactly that.

"I wrote a book called *The Art of Non-Conformity* when I was first starting," Chris said. "I went on the road to all fifty states and met readers everywhere, doing my own little book tour. In some places, there would be fifty people and other places there would be five, and that was cool. I knew right from the beginning there was something special about my community – *the* community, not just mine. They're awesome people, and I wanted to do anything I could to connect them.

"It's awesome to see great people in L.A. or Portland, but there are awesome people all over the world. I wanted to bring them together. The initial idea of my annual event was to do an in-person gathering. We didn't make it all about entrepreneurship, even though there were a lot of entrepreneurs there. And we didn't make it all about travel, even though there were a lot of active travelers. Or arts, or education. Our thinking was, *Let's just bring together like-minded people who share these values.* The values we ended up with were community, adventure, and service. It was very organic. We didn't know what we were doing. We didn't know anything about running events. And maybe that was for the better in the long-run. The first year was hard in terms of logistics and getting overcharged for things, and not knowing how to do production and all that stuff, but if you have the fundamentals right – if you have the right people – then you can figure out all that stuff later. So we grew from there."

There are More Options and Possibilities Than Meet the Eye

I sent several emails to Chris, and I love the fact that he's responded to every single one. That's a mark of authenticity – someone who cares enough about their readers to respond to them.

"If plan 'A' fails – remember you have 25 letters left," Chris said.

We often get so hung up on a single way *having* to work that we miss additional options and possibilities. This mirrors what successful entrepreneur Suzanne Duret will share with us later in the book. To share a recent example from my life – used as a means to help make the point – I once again competed in the Toastmasters International Speech Contest in 2014. After competing against some of the best speakers from across the Northeast of the United States, and coming in first place, I flew to Kuala Lumpur, Malaysia, to compete in the semifinals of the World Championship of Public Speaking. I didn't win, but I came close to becoming the youngest speaking champion in history. I then used that as a springboard to start speaking professionally and getting paid for it.

Since 2014, I've grown and evolved as a speaker, and I've gotten better. Naturally, one would assume that would mean I would do even better in the speech contest, like winning the semifinals or even becoming the World Champion of Public Speaking. But in 2016 I lost at the district level, coming in third place. This was an accomplishment unto itself, but it's a level below the caliber of competition I squared off against in Kuala Lumpur in 2014. I was a good sport and congratulated the winner, but on the inside, I couldn't help but feel disappointed.

With all of that said, since 2014 I've also grown enormously as a person. I've built a strong foundation as a professional speaker, and my horizons have significantly broadened. Chris's words of wisdom ring true in my psyche now more than ever – the Toastmasters speech contest was only one path among many to share my message with the world. There are TEDx talks, YouTube interviews, guest blogging opportunities, speaking at companies, speaking at schools, and that's all just the tip of the iceberg.

I used that example as a vehicle to make a point that will benefit you as you face your own setbacks and disappointments. Remember that there are all sorts of options, possibilities, combinations, and permutations as to the path you can take. Don't let one setback stop you from seeing all the other choices available to you.

Increasing optionality also applies to your career. "It's better to be at the bottom of the ladder you want to climb than to be on the top of one you don't," Chris said. Realize that you can absolutely transition into a different job or career if the one you are in isn't right for you! Don't do anything impulsive; think your choices through based on your life situation, but remember there are more possibilities than you may initially realize.

We often get stuck in jobs and careers that we hate, but we feel we have to do them. I've been there, but I also know what it's like to transition into a career that's better for you. *I've lived this.* I totally understand the need to grind and pay the bills, but what I'm saying to you is the same thing Chris is saying: expand your horizons, start hustling, and start applying to new jobs and careers. If you don't have work experience that matches the job you are seeking, then use the extracurricular organizations you are a part of to sell yourself. If you are not a part of any extracurricular organizations, then consider joining a Toastmasters, Rotary, Lions, Kiwanis, or Chamber of Commerce club. I've literally gotten jobs because of my experience as a speaker, even though I've never officially spoken in a "job" – my paid speaking engagements have all been through my own initiatives and business dealings.

I'm *not* saying to suddenly quit your current job for no reason. I'm suggesting you think outside the box and creatively leverage your talents and strengths to place yourself in a better situation in the near future than you are right now. Stop putting your happiness off to *someday*. Realize someday is today and take massive action.

Every "Somebody" Was Once a "Nobody"

We often see an extremely successful person and think to ourselves, *I wish I could do that, but I'm not as connected as they are.* Here's the kicker: Everyone who now has a lot of connections started out as a no-name with no connections. We all start off as nobodies. Don't let the lie of society, and the media's incessant brainwashing, make you think that some people are more worthy than you. No one is better than you, no one is above you, and everyone is your equal. Yes, someone may be ahead of you financially or career-wise, but that doesn't mean they are better than you.

"Never despise small beginnings," Chris said, "and don't belittle your own accomplishments. Remember them and use them as inspiration as you go on to the next thing. When you venture outside your comfort zone, wherever the starting point may be, it's kind of a big deal."

Stop comparing yourself to others! As successful entrepreneur and speaker Kinja Dixon said in an Instagram post, this is *your* journey and no one else's. Who cares if someone is "ahead" of you? There was never anything to compare to begin with, as you are infinitely unique. Let me say it again: This is *your* journey. My friend Kinja was speaking overseas, and his message to the audience ties right into Chris's wisdom: Give yourself credit for moving forward and making progress, regardless of your starting point or where you may find yourself right now. You're doing better than you think you are, and you're farther along than you realize.

Give Yourself Permission to Hustle

I was reading Chris's bestselling book *The $100 Startup: Reinvent the Way You Make a Living, Do What You Love, and Create a New Future* and I came across a very powerful passage I felt compelled to share.

"A charlatan is all talk, with nothing to back up their claims," Chris said. "A martyr is all action with plenty of good work to talk about, but remains unable or unwilling to do the talking. A hustler represents the ideal combination: work and talk fused together.

"Being willing to promote in an authentic, non-sleazy manner is a core attribute of microbusiness success. Sometimes the best hustling lies in creating a great offer and getting people to talk about it. In other cases, you want to have as many of the right kind of customers as possible, so there's nothing wrong with putting yourself forward."

The reason I had to share this is that there are people in the world who think that promoting yourself is a bad thing. This is simply not true. If you've written a book, created a product, or put into place some sort of service that adds value to others, choosing to not promote it will actually cause you a lack of success. Chris's insight shows us that when we strike the perfect balance between hard work and promotion, we find the happy medium of hustle that allows us to achieve success.

Notice also a key aspect of what Chris said above: *Being willing to promote in an authentic, non-sleazy manner.* In order to leverage the power of authentic leadership you must be willing to promote yourself, but make sure you do it in a genuine way that demonstrates how what you do helps others.

Persistence

Before we leave this chapter, I'd also like to add an insight from my friend and fellow author Heather Hansen O'Neill which complements our discussion. Heather is a leadership expert. We were chatting over breakfast at a diner one morning in Newtown, Connecticut and I told Heather that I often get discouraged when I repeatedly email potential clients but don't hear back.

"Don't let that get to you or discourage you," Heather said. "I once boldly introduced myself to a conference organizer at a conference I wasn't speaking at. She was friendly in person and seemed interested, but she didn't respond to any of my emails. Over the course of a year, I sent her seven follow-up emails. One day, one of her assistants offered me a paid speaking engagement. In fact, it was one of the most lucrative paid speaking engagements of my entire life. Had I been afraid to follow-up with her, or if I let the discouragement of her lack of reply get to me, I never would have been at the forefront of her mind when she ended up hiring me to speak."

This is incredibly inspirational. I share this because you may have the hustle part down, but if you are anything like me you get discouraged and upset when people ignore you. The worst – and I'm experiencing this right now – is when someone is super-friendly, engaging, and interested in your services in person, but then they go radio silent on you despite your repeated follow-ups.

Let's use this wisdom and advice to springboard to the next level of our careers and lives. To be clear, this doesn't mean you have to repeatedly follow-up with *everyone* (for example, a friend who doesn't respond to you after two or three contact attempts may be best left alone), but from a business point of view, this is brilliant. You can be authentic and persistent at the same time. Don't be afraid to respectfully follow-up with people and remind them of what you do, especially when they may have initially ignored you.

Hustle + Persistence = Success

Chapter 7: Get Out of Your Head Space and Liberate Yourself

"When you get into a tight place, and everything goes against you, till it seems as though you could not hang on a minute longer, never give up then, for that is just the place and time that the tide will turn."
– Harriet Beecher Stowe

My phone conversation with successful entrepreneur Suzanne Duret was awesome, to say the least. We had mutual friends on Facebook and soon became Facebook friends ourselves. I felt a great vibe from her through the online world, so we decided to continue the relationship and conversation in person.

I'm genuinely pleased to say we met through Facebook because I'm happy something so positive came from that platform. Some people will tell you to stay off social media completely, and some people will tell you to use social media all the time. I fall somewhere in-between those two extremes: While social media definitely has its downside and is addictive in nature, it also can be a truly wonderful way to stay in touch with people and make new connections. I just completed a self-imposed hiatus from social media that lasted for more than three months – I definitely will take breaks from social media, but I also know it is a powerful platform and certainly has its uses. Be mindful of your social media habits and use those platforms appropriately.

Take Initiative and Just Do It

Suzanne made it big as an entrepreneur in the medical device field, partnering with a doctor. I asked her how she got started in entrepreneurship.

"I was working in Minnesota as a secretary," Suzanne said. "I knew I wanted to advance my career, and ultimately I wanted to be an entrepreneur, but I had to figure out how. It so happened that my boss was starting a new real estate development project in Florida and he had recently bought a huge yacht that he kept there. He decided to send the receptionist and me to Florida for a week's vacation as a thank you for all of our great work. The first day we were on the yacht drinking champagne and eating delicious food; it was amazing. I was on the yacht for a day, but the next day I realized I didn't want to spend my week doing nothing other than partying. I decided to create my own opportunity.

"I spent the rest of the week visiting with people that were contracted to work on my boss's new development project. I spent time at the construction site, and I investigated the small city, asking people relevant questions. I discovered weak spots in the operation and learned that the key manager was actually doing some pretty shifty things behind my boss's back.

"When the vacation was over on my first day back to the Minnesota office, I sat down with my boss and laid out exactly what I discovered, including my insights and recommendations for improvements. I explained how my boss needed someone he could trust to keep an eye on things and report to him, due to integrity issues with his key manager. I also explained everything I learned about the growth of the town and the many opportunities from a development standpoint. My boss was absolutely blown away with my initiative and what I was showing him. The next day he decided to triple my salary and relocate me down to Florida as his trusted office manager, reporting directly to him."

"It's amazing that you did that," I said to Suzanne, "and an incredibly impressive story. Your initiative is inspirational. So when you were in Florida on the second day you literally just showed up on-site at the Florida office?"

"Yes, exactly that," Suzanne said. "I showed up, introduced myself, and started asking good questions. By asking questions and talking to lots of different people, I was able to find the holes in the operation and found out about the shady dealings of his main on-site manager, which is what enabled me to add so much value to my boss when I told him what was happening.

"At first I doubted myself, but then I told myself to just go for it. One of the big keys to success is to get out of your head space and take action."

By "head space," Suzanne is referring to the way we get caught up in our own minds through self-doubt, over-analysis, and self-sabotaging limiting behaviors. I know this state of mind as well as anybody. Suzanne is telling us to literally stop the doubts by saying to ourselves; *I'm just going to do it.*

"Whenever self-doubts come," Suzanne said, "I envision a big red circle with an X through it, and that reminds me to instantly stop self-doubt and negative thoughts from affecting my behavior. The moment you waste time doubting yourself to the point where it prevents you from taking action is the moment you're done."

One of the keys to prosperity is to get out of your head space and take action in spite of your doubts. Rather than sitting around thinking about why you can't or shouldn't be doing it, just do it.

Liberate Yourself and Let Go of What You Think is Supposed to Happen

"You've been able to create and manifest so much in your life and business," I said to Suzanne. "How did you do it, and how do you continue to do it?"

"First I always trust my intuition. Second, I set the right kind of intention for a goal I have," Suzanne said. "And then I just LET GO of it. I don't pray on it, I don't meditate on it, I don't do vision boards, and all that stuff people do. When you have a goal, and you are looking at a vision board all day, it's almost like doubting yourself. It might cause you to think, *What if I don't do it? What if I don't achieve the goal?"* Instead, I set the intention for my goal, and then I let go of dwelling on it and just take action on doing things to get me there. It's like if you feel you have to keep praying the same prayer over and over – you are showing that you don't have faith that your very first prayer was heard. Trying to keep visualizing or meditating over and over is very similar. If you really have faith in yourself and your outcome, you only need to set the intent once, have faith, and take action. Period."

"This is resonating with me very deeply right now," I said to Suzanne. "A lot of people out there will tell you to have vision boards, and I've done all sorts of goal affirmations constantly throughout the day. It became too much. It was almost like the more I did it, the less I trusted that it would actually happen. I'm a fan of visualization, but the trick is to do a brief visualization and then let it go, rather than obsessing and worrying about the goal all day."

"Exactly," Suzanne said. "Absolutely be sure to set a clear intention, and definitely believe in yourself 100%. What I'm saying here is rather than get caught up in your head and in all sorts of vision board exercises, go out into the world, start taking action, and simply trust it will happen.

"It's about *not* needing or requiring it to happen in a certain way or timeframe, with a certain person or group of people, or in a certain kind of situation. If you are caught up in it happening in a certain kind of way, you might miss the opportunity that could make your desire come true. Things may not happen in the way you initially expect, and if you are rigidly tied to the way you think it's supposed to happen, you will limit yourself."

"This is very helpful insight," I said to Suzanne. "You're really hitting the nail right on the head. Can you give an example of what you're talking about?"

"A great example," Suzanne said, "is one of the times when I was looking for angel investors to fund one of my business ventures. I had created a list of people that could potentially invest, and I was preparing to approach all of them. But one day I was chatting with my hairdresser about my startup business, and she told me about a wealthy guy she knew. Something told me I needed to talk to the guy, so I asked her to get him on the phone right then and there while I was with her. She called him, introduced me, then handed the phone to me. I had a 10-minute phone call with this guy, and the rest became history. He not only ended up becoming my biggest investor, but he also brought all of the other investors in as well. I never even had a chance to approach the people on my original list. If I were tied to the way I thought it was supposed to all happen, I would have completely missed the opportunity that the universe placed in my lap. Instead of head tripping about things, I trusted my instincts and just jumped in by taking action."

This is incredibly powerful content and insight. In a lot of personal development books you'll read about vision boards, but here we're offering you a different, more freeing approach to life. This is not a shortcut or easy way out, as you still need to put in the hard work. It's about reducing your stress as an authentic leader, so you have the mental energy needed to take action and deal with the challenges of daily life. A quick example from my own life involves the Toastmasters International Speech Contest, a once-a-year contest where speakers compete in an effort to become the World Champion of Public Speaking. In 2014 I became the District 53 Champion, competing against the best speakers from across the Northeast and winning. I went on to compete in Kuala Lumpur, Malaysia and I lost at the semifinals level but was excited to compete again in 2015. This is the same general contest I referred to earlier in the chapter featuring Chris Guillebeau, but I'm now referring to the 2015 contest instead of the 2016 contest. I'm also highlighting a different lesson.

In 2015, I was gung-ho set on becoming the International Speaking Champion. I did meditations, visualizations, affirmations, and practiced my butt off. I ended up getting third place at the District level, which was disappointing and seemed like a step backward from my previous year's achievement. But there was a high school teacher in the audience who liked my speaking style and ended up bringing me in to speak to all 800 students at the high school he taught at, one of the most epic speaking engagements of my life up until that point in time.

First of all, getting third at the District level is an achievement, not a failure. Part of my growth as a person came in realizing that even though I fell short of the ridiculously high bar I set for myself, I could still be satisfied with my effort. After all, I did my absolute best. Second, judging in Toastmasters is subjective (this is not at all putting down the well-deserved winner of the contest, but rather acknowledging that there is a strong human element to Toastmasters' contests) – the contest is more about growing as a speaker than it is winning. Third, something bigger came out of the contest for me in keynote speaking to an entire high school, which is what I truly wanted to do in the first place! Intention and desire are good but don't get so caught up on the way things are "supposed" to be that you miss the gift life is handing you. Liberate yourself from the binds of being constantly insecure about whether or not you'll achieve your goal, and adopt a more free-flowing, action-oriented approach. Your results and peace of mind will astound you.

The Power of Authenticity

Suzanne was able to inspire Tony Robbins to write the foreword to her book. She didn't know Tony or anyone else who knew him. So Suzanne decided to do her research and find someone close to Tony who she could connect with for an introduction. Through a series of phone calls, she connected with one of Tony's right-hand men, named Roger. Suzanne was able to motivate Roger to have lunch with her when he came to her town, and during that lunch, she helped Roger to see the value of Tony writing the foreword to her book. Suzanne was there to serve and talked about what she was going to do for Tony, not what she wanted Tony to do for her. In the end, Roger made sure Suzanne got personal time with Tony when he came to town for his live event. And because Suzanne was focused on how she was going to serve Tony, she was able to achieve her goal of having Tony write the foreword to her book. This demonstrates how Suzanne effectively got face time with a very successful person by using her intelligence, creativity, and authenticity to serve others while also serving herself.

"Tell me more about how you got started," I said to Suzanne. "Your entrepreneurial journey is fascinating, and I want to know more about how you used authenticity to drive your success."

"Well, because I didn't have a college degree I felt inadequate, and I used to hide behind a mask," Suzanne said. "I was a chameleon in the sense that I would change my approach and personality based on the kinds of people I happened to be with. It seemed like a good strategy, but at the end of the day, I wasn't happy with myself. I eventually got tired of trying to be someone else and made a promise to myself that I'd be authentic from then on out."

As Suzanne knows, it's not a good feeling to be someone you're not. If you are fake for a long period of time, there might come a day where you look in the mirror and don't know who you are anymore. Here's an important point to remember: It's okay for someone to not like you, as long as they don't like you because you were being *you.* There's nothing worse than someone not liking you for being someone you're not.

As I talked about in one of my previous books, *Reach Your Mountaintop*, I had a difficult time in high school. Although I wasn't to blame for the hurtful and cruel actions of the people I went to school with, it is worth pointing out one of my core flaws and errors: I constantly wore a mask. I wore the mask of trying to be someone I wasn't, and the mask of trying to keep everyone happy except myself. This included pretending like everything was alright even though I was seriously depressed. A big part of transforming my life after this difficult experience was taking off the mask and being myself with others. It didn't instantly solve all my problems, but over time it did lead to more genuine connections. Best of all, I was able to show my true self to the world and be liked (or disliked) *for who I really am*. I share this to encourage you to take off the mask, and keep off the mask, at all times. I'm using examples from my life as a vehicle to give you the lessons I learned the hard way. This is about you and your success, and if you apply these tips in your life, you will reap the rewards.

"When I was starting my first venture," Suzanne said, "my business partner and I met with a couple of tough venture capitalists. This was in my early days as an entrepreneur in my mid-twenties. Because I felt inadequate not having a college degree, I would try to make myself look smarter by wearing a very concealing suit and putting my hair up. I tried to look overly professional because a lot of men found me to be attractive and I was trying to take the emphasis off my looks. The conversation was going well as the VCs interviewed my business partner, who was a medical doctor and the inventor of our medical devices. He was brilliant in his area of expertise but lacked social and business skills. That's where I came in. And then it was time to interview me. The lead VC turned to me and made an *extremely* inappropriate sexual statement, based on the fact that he considered me to be attractive. Being attractive and young, without a college degree, made me a sitting duck for not being taken seriously by business people, especially men.

"When the VC made his offensive comment, I was shocked! But I had a nanosecond of seeing the shift in his body language right before he spoke, so I knew something was coming and I was prepared. I could have reacted angrily or aggressively, or fallen apart and started crying like he was probably anticipating. Instead, I calmly told him I didn't appreciate his statement. Then, I packed up my briefcase, reached across the table to shake his hand, smiled, thanked him for his time, and left the room. I didn't flinch. I didn't get sucked into reacting. I didn't allow myself to be taken advantage of or disrespected. A few days went by, and the venture capitalist called me on the phone. He said he was very impressed with how I handled myself and explained that his crude words were meant to test me. He said that I passed the test and they wanted to make an investment. He offered the full $1.2 million in funding we needed. I explained that there were many ways he could have tested me without being so disrespectful. I said no to his funding offer. I had to stay true to myself and trust that the right investors would show up. I wasn't going to put myself, or my business, into the hands of someone that had already shown me what type of person he was. And of course as things go, we did, in fact, raise all of the funding from another VC group, and they were all complete gentlemen that had our best interests at heart."

"Wow," I said. "I give you an enormous amount of credit for not buying into his games and staying true to yourself. That's pure authenticity right there."

"Yes," Suzanne said. "I refused to do business with someone who thought it was alright to treat and talk to me that way, regardless of how much money he was offering my company. I stayed true to myself about the kinds of people I wanted to deal with, despite the allure of money. You attract people in accordance to how you treat yourself and others."

Let's think about and process this for a second. I'm not talking about Suzanne turning down a hundred, a thousand, or even ten thousand dollars. *She turned down over a million dollars, and she did it respectfully despite the disrespect she received.* Suzanne is the epitome of activating the power of authentic leadership in her life, demonstrating two core themes of this book: 1) She maintained kindness. It's important to be respectful to others, as you never know what someone may be going through. 2) Being authentic means "sticking to your guns" even when it's hard to do. Let's make something crystal clear: Being authentic does NOT mean folding over for someone, being a people pleaser, and letting others treat you like garbage. Being authentic means doing what's right for you, even when other people disagree with your choice and decision. Suzanne is the perfect demonstration of this. And you're going to love what she tells us next.

Have the Guts to Be Who You Really Are

Suzanne Duret has guts, to say the least. This is a key quality of authenticity: Having the guts to be yourself and look past labels, no matter what situation you find yourself in. Things were not always easy for Suzanne. In fact, sometimes they were downright nearly impossible.

"I've had many nights curled into the fetal position, slamming my fists out of fear and frustration," Suzanne said. "Starting a business is tough, and I've started many. I've learned that when people are faced with financial stress or opportunities for greed, many will change for the worse. They become someone else, someone ugly, someone who is no longer true to themselves and others. I actually had to sue someone I had known and worked with for over twenty years because greed got the best of him, and he didn't want to pay my 6-figure commission on a deal. When people stop being who they really are because of certain circumstances, it's horribly destructive, especially for the person who changed their behavior."

But even as all of this was happening, Suzanne maintained her authenticity. She ended up forgiving this gentleman after they settled out of court. Because of Suzanne's desire to not become someone she isn't due to this circumstance, she and the gentleman she had to sue have put it behind them and gone on to remain friends.

As Suzanne moved on to starting another new business and looking for different investors, she was again faced with remaining true to being her authentic self.

"I landed a meeting with the founder of a very well-known company," Suzanne said. "He was one of those guys everyone looked up to, and also feared," Suzanne said. "He was intimidating in the sense that he was extremely successful and answered to no one. He's one of those guys you never mess with because he is known to have a temper.

"We met at his house so I could pitch him on my investment opportunity. During the conversation, I didn't treat him any differently than anyone else at the meeting. Instead, *I chose to be myself* and treat everyone on an equal playing field. There were other prospective investors in attendance, but they didn't have the high-level of status that Mr. Big Shot did. After making my pitch, Mr. Big Shot offered to fund the entire $1.4 million right there on the spot – but he wanted 75% of my company instead of the 20% I had structured. Everyone else in the room freaked out, as they wanted to share in the investment opportunity too. I stood my ground and very calmly explained that I would not accept the offer. I explained again what my investment terms were, and that I wasn't going to give up 75% of my company or deny the opportunity for others in the room to participate in the funding of my new business. Although what I said was delivered in a calm and rational way, Mr. Big Shot was taken aback that I was so direct and unwavering with him, especially because very few, if any, ever talked to him that way. I could see by looking around the room that I had gained instant respect from all of the others because I stayed true to who I am and to my deal structure, and I was mindful of others in the room that deserved an opportunity to participate. Because I'm so grounded in my integrity and belief that I will reach my goals without having to compromise myself or others, I had no hesitation or fear in responding the way I did to that gentleman's offer."

This is where Suzanne's integrity and authenticity really shine through: No one would have blamed her for compromising on her values a little bit in order to get funding that quickly and easily. But she stayed true to herself even when she had an opportunity not to. She's an incredible role model and example for us. *Suzanne didn't let the circumstances of her life situation change or compromise the person she is.*

Suzanne went on to share, "That successful Mr. Big Shot whom I was so direct with didn't respond angrily or in a hostile way to me, but he clearly wasn't pleased. I could tell I caught him off guard. Others in attendance ended up investing in my company over the next week. Meanwhile, Mr. Big Shot would only communicate with me through his attorney in order to make an investment. That's right – he still invested, but a smaller amount at the same terms as everyone else."

Do you see how powerful authenticity can be, as Suzanne just demonstrated? By staying true to your authenticity in the present moment, you ensure your peace of mind in the long-run. Also, you attract the right people into your life. Suzanne's directness was why she attracted the right investors on her terms – they all respected that she handled things with integrity and didn't change who she was to satisfy the biggest investor in the group.

Why I love this story so much, and why Suzanne's personality is a great match for this book, is because she made it a point to be authentic no matter what. This created long-term happiness for herself as well as genuine sustainability for her business. How many people would have compromised themselves to get money from that intimidating investor Suzanne met with? Countless people would have, and I don't blame them, but it's not a sustainable way of operating in this world. A lot of people have values and morals, but only to a certain extent. I say this with all due respect, but when times get tough, some people will change who they are in a heartbeat. People will turn into animals, but hopefully, Suzanne's example will help prevent many of you from doing so in the future.

Have you ever seen someone go from happy to angry or frustrated within a short period of time? If you say the wrong thing, they become upset and easily offended. When you can't be yourself around someone, you know that person is not right for you. For the record, there are times when it is appropriate to get upset with someone, like if they've broken a promise or betrayed you. But what I'm referring to here is when people get mad at you for no good reason. Some people will get hostile because you decided to assert or stand up for yourself in a genuine way. These are bad eggs; people who pretend to have respect for you, but deep down don't think highly of you.

"Your stories express exactly the message I'm looking to get across," I said to Suzanne. "I know for me and my style as a writer and speaker, I wear my heart on my sleeve. I'm very transparent and open about everything I've experienced, with the purpose of benefiting others with the lessons I wish I would have learned sooner. Some people love this about me. And some people don't like it at all. When I did my book launch for my previous book, *Reach Your Mountaintop,* on November 1st of 2016, the one you read and endorsed me for, I was extremely transparent about my absolute rock bottom moment. A lot of people supported the message and shared it. And a couple of people de-friended me on Facebook. You know what I've realized though? It doesn't matter if some people don't like it. The message isn't for them. The message is for the people who need to hear it, the people who are meant to benefit from it."

"That's spot on," Suzanne said. "And exactly right. I read your entire book, and I was blown away and impressed by your level of authenticity. You bared your soul. For many people that style is going to work. And for some, it may not. For me, too, there are people who say I'm not their cup of tea. But that's not my problem. There are people who really resonate with what I have to share, and I focus on those people. If someone doesn't like me, that's their problem, not mine."

Did you catch what Suzanne said just now? *There are people who really resonate with what she has to share, and she focuses on those people.* A big fault of mine throughout my life is that I would focus on the few haters instead of the many supporters. If I put out a video on YouTube or Facebook and twenty people like it, but one person says it's a horrible video, at the end of the day I would feel bothered by the one person who didn't like it. However, I know I'm progressing because the other day someone left a negative comment to me on YouTube, and I laughed about it instead of letting it bring me down. If you don't find yourself being able to perfectly live these tips right away, don't beat yourself up. That's normal – I, and many others, have been there. Give yourself credit for making an effort, an effort that most people don't ever make, and then keep moving forward. Keep applying these principles, and you'll get better at them. If I, Jeff Davis, the king of taking things personally, can get better at it, then I'm certain you can as well.

Give Yourself Permission to Change Your Mind (for the Right Reasons)

Suzanne has talked to us about liberating ourselves from the bonds of the "should's," "must's," and "have to's," instead choosing to freely move toward our goals with genuine intention but without attachment or worry. Remind yourself daily that while no one owes you anything, you also don't owe other people anything. I'd like to share with you how these principles have led to liberation in my own life.

After my mother's 6- and 7-year-old students were tragically, senselessly, and unthinkably murdered at my old elementary school, (Sandy Hook Elementary School) – and after I spent many months trying to process what happened (I, like many others, still haven't fully processed what happened) – I became determined to climb Mount Everest in honor of their lives. I started talking to many professional mountain climbers, I looked into sponsors by filling out lengthy application forms online, and I went so far as to walk into banks and ask the managers for funding. Like Suzanne, I also have some guts.

Climbing Mount Everest is incredibly expensive, so I knew I had to not only save lots of money but also figure out how to make a quantum leap in my funding – that's why I approached potential sponsors while also pushing really hard to further grow my business.

While doing all of this, in September of 2015, I found out extremely popular and successful blogger Scott Dinsmore tragically died due to a fluke accident while climbing Mount Kilimanjaro. Climbing Mount Kilimanjaro is less difficult than climbing Mount Everest, but due to unexpected falling boulders outside of Scott's control, this amazing man's life was unfairly taken. This incident really shook me up and caused me to wonder if I truly wanted to risk losing my life in my twenties in an attempt to ascend to the top of Mount Everest. (Quick sidebar: Feel free to check out some of Scott's YouTube videos and blog posts, as he was a true gift to this planet and filled with endless amounts of wisdom. His website is *liveyourlegend.net*.)

Further, I was also working on several initiatives for my business, including traveling to new countries and launching my 2nd book, *Reach Your Mountaintop.* (The book has nothing to do with mountain climbing; it's about reaching your own version of success. The image of the mountain is a metaphor for ascending your own chosen career and life path.) After careful reflection, with all of these factors going through my mind at once, I decided not to pursue climbing Mount Everest as my number one goal in life.

Sounds simple enough, right? Not at all. I'm the kind of person who will do something if I said I'll do it. I had said on one of my YouTube videos that I was going to climb Mount Everest to honor my mom's students who were now passed away. I really, seriously, truly struggled with this for many months and years. I felt like I was letting both myself and others down. Even though I knew climbing Mount Everest was not the right thing to do at this point in my life, there was a large part of me that felt like I was coming up short.

After talking to several close friends about it and really digging deep into my psyche as to why I felt this way about myself, I had an epiphany: *Choosing not to do something is not the same as compromising on your integrity and character.* The feeling was real, but the why behind the feeling was a lie! The feeling of not being good enough was real, but why I felt this way is because I thought I was compromising on something that I promised to someone else. With that said, the epiphany I had was that I wasn't compromising on my values or letting someone else down. Here's the thing: I didn't promise someone that I'd climb Mount Everest. Yes, I had put it out to the world that I would climb Everest, and at that moment in time I said it with 100% full authenticity – I was, after all, making serious strides to make it happen. But I also have a right to change my mind, as long as I'm changing my mind for the *right reasons*. And I was – I had other initiatives going on that I was moving forward with, and I also didn't want a tragedy to happen in my twenties when there were other ways I could help people.

To further help me along my path of liberation, I also had a heart-to-heart conversation with Rick Cleri, a digital marketing expert and successful business owner we'll hear more from later in this book. Rick said to me, "Jeff, don't feel like you *have* to climb Mount Everest. If it doesn't reflect where you're going with your life right now, then don't do it."

I liberated myself by realizing that it's okay to not climb Mount Everest because not doing so was *not* compromising on my values. The decision simply reflected where I was at in my life and business, and what risk-tolerance I was willing to put up with. I was harder on myself about the whole thing than anyone else was, and when I finally eased up on myself, I found the peace and freedom I desired.

My own evolution as a person has led me to realize that just because you said you were going to do something yesterday doesn't mean you have to do it today if doing it today doesn't reflect your best interests. In my case, I made a declaration to the world, and for a while, I felt I was obligated to climb Mount Everest because of that declaration. But then I set myself free by realizing I was allowed to change my direction as I saw fit. If you do make a promise to someone about something, and you later regret making that promise, go to the person directly and be as transparent and straight forward as possible. Tell them you will not best serve yourself, or them, by doing something that you don't want to do. A reasonable and respectful person will understand and find someone else. If the person doesn't respect you for coming to them in transparency, they most likely weren't someone you wanted to work or spend time with anyway. If the obligation is something you or someone else feels you absolutely must do, then do it. But learn from it, and be more careful of the promises you make in the future. Don't leave people hanging high and dry – go to them with your concerns and talk it through with them.

Will I climb Mount Everest later in my life? It's absolutely possible, and not out of the question. But not right now. And I'm continuing to speak on leadership, anti-bullying, and overcoming adversity to high schools, colleges, conferences, associations, and businesses around the world.

"You are honoring your mother's students by being yourself," my girlfriend said to me. "You are honoring your mother's students by the way you authentically share your story with the world. That, in itself, is enough."

That comment from my girlfriend, along with these wonderful insights from Suzanne and Rick, helped me enormously, as for the longest time I felt like I wasn't good enough. **Part of being authentic means giving yourself permission to change direction when the time is right to do so. You are enough, exactly as you are.** If what you said a day ago, a week ago, a month ago, a year ago, or a decade ago no longer reflects your true desires, then give yourself permission to change course. Just make sure your reasons for changing course are legitimate, genuine, and standing on a firm foundation of integrity. While you are being consistent and following through on your promises to yourself and others, also know that it's completely alright to pick a new course of action. Liberate yourself with the power of your authenticity and your potential will soar.

Chapter 8: Use Authenticity to Deal With Difficult Challenges

"There are over three billion people in the world who go to bed hungry for something to eat every night, but over five billion people go to bed every night hungry for a kind word, a sincere compliment, a word of encouragement."
– Cavett Robert

You may have thought what we heard from Evan Carmichael earlier was all we were going to hear from him. Absolutely not! This YouTube star is filled with valuable content and has more to offer us on how we can use authenticity to deal with difficult challenges.

Get Excited When You Hit Rock Bottom

"What do you suggest someone do when they hit rock bottom," I asked Evan, "and when they feel like there is no way out? I'm talking about that time when they've been knocked down time and time again, and they feel stuck. They've reached the end of their rope, and after many setbacks, they are now at rock bottom."

"Get excited," Evan said with a big smile. "I love the rock bottom. The rock bottom setback means something big is coming. I think back to my own rock bottom moment. I had a software company making almost nothing, like 300 dollars a month, and I felt absolutely worthless. I was working on it day in and day out, and I was getting no results whatsoever.

"My rock bottom moment was when I told my partner I quit. Hearing those words come out of my mouth was devastating. I woke up the day after feeling 100% worthless knowing that something in my life wasn't working.

"The next day, I knew I couldn't quit and wanted to keep doing this. But I knew I needed to find a different way to do it. That's what is so great about the rock bottom moment. It forces you to find a different way to stand. It challenges you to ask yourself, *Should I be doing this or not? Is it worth the headache and anguish? Or should I be doing something else?* For me, I knew I needed to keep doing this, I just had to find another way to stand.

"I realized that someone has already figured this out. I knew I had to model someone. That's when I modeled myself after Bill Gates, and that was the beginning of the turnaround for me. Rock bottom forces you to ask yourself tough questions and make important changes, which is usually the beginning of something better.

"I had a friend who was in a really bad relationship with a girl. It took him an entire year to get out of that extremely tough situation. But when he finally broke up with her, he went and did courageous things. He went dancing. He went and lived his life. He felt free. Even though it came from something really bad and one of the worst moments of his life, it forced a change for him in a positive direction.

"A big problem for a lot of people is that their minor setbacks aren't big enough. If you get a major setback it really forces you to look in the mirror. So if you have a big setback, get excited."

"I love that," I said. "Something that I share with a lot of my audiences is that there's a hidden opportunity in every setback, and you mirrored that directly. You mentioned how you had that turning point – when you quit your business and had to find a new way to stand. You knew you didn't want to permanently quit the industry and you found a better way to operate. I find that to be very powerful. Can you talk about that a little more?"

"One of the challenges I had with my business is feeling like I had to come up with every idea myself," Evan said. "I'm the entrepreneur, I'm the creative person – I felt like I had to come up with all of it myself. At first, I didn't have an answer. All I knew was that my old way wasn't working. That in itself is liberating – recognizing that you need to do something totally different because the way you're doing it now isn't working.

"That's when I modeled myself after Bill Gates, and after a few weeks, I saw results. Momentum. Sales. *Something*. Something to eat. When you're starving, an apple is the most luxurious meal in the world. I'd like to emphasize that the turning point was knowing that what I was doing wasn't working. It's not a tweak I needed to change – it had to be a revolution, something totally different. Tweaking was what I was already doing, and it wasn't working. Tweaking is what led me to the crash. I needed a wholesale change in my approach. That's what led to the rise up."

Cutting Out Overwhelm Before It Even Happens

"There are so many people who are overwhelmed in the world," I said to Evan. "They're overworked, and they feel like there's too much to do and not enough time. They feel like they have an endless amount of obligations and not enough 'me' time. Do you ever feel overwhelmed? You are a content machine, always putting out new content. If you do feel overwhelmed, how do you deal with it?"

"It starts with the awareness that it's all self-inflicted," Evan said. "You choose what you're doing. Take responsibility for your schedule. You might say, *Yes, well my boss wants me to do this.* Well, you chose to work there. And you chose not to speak up about the situation. There's always an option.

"With any challenge you're facing, you need to accept the personal responsibility that's on you to get out of it. Most people just default to complaining. You blame your wife, you blame your kids, you blame your parents, you blame your boss, you blame the President, and it's always somebody else's fault. Because complaining feels good. You don't want to do the hard work of actually doing something about it and changing the situation.

"That's why it starts with the awareness of knowing it's self-inflicted. The solution comes from knowing you have the power to get out of it. The way I deal with overwhelm is by constantly evaluating my schedule and my time. For me, the hardest part isn't being overwhelmed. It's being willing to let go of things that are good. If it sucked, it would be easy to drop it. But if it's good, it may not be as easy to drop. It's not amazing, but it's not horrible. The key is to develop the courage to leave the 'good' behind and go for something better. Good keeps you in your comfort zone. Good keeps you safe. Good provides an income. Good keeps you where you are, but it doesn't push you forward.

"I'm constantly asking myself, *Am I doing something great? Is this activity worth it*? I use my schedule a lot. If I feel like I don't have enough time to do something that I really want to do, that's when I know I need to make a change. I'm constantly evaluating my schedule. I recently took on a new business opportunity that takes up five hours per week. I didn't take that on and leave everything else how it was; I took on the new opportunity and dedicated Tuesdays to it. I then took the 'good' activities I was doing on Tuesdays and eliminated them from my schedule.

"I don't allow myself to get overwhelmed. I do that by not letting things build up. For a lot of people, it's the buildup that gets them. For six months straight, you let someone else dictate your schedule. For six months straight, you let things slide. As soon as I start to feel a little bit of it, I adjust my schedule immediately. This is what cuts out overwhelm for me. I allow what I'm doing to serve me, which means letting go of some things that don't serve me and a higher purpose."

Make the Change

"That's excellent," I said. "Making changes and letting go of good is very important, as good can be the enemy of great. What would you say to someone who is in a job they don't like? They're not yet a full-time entrepreneur, but they still need a job to pay the bills. Would you tell them to get a job better suited for them first?"

"First off I'd ask them if they really want to be an entrepreneur. If that's their heart's desire and something they truly want to do, I'd tell them to go work for someone who already has done what they want to do. Get as close to the sun as you possibly can. For example, if I wanted to be a TEDx speaker and write three books I'd want to learn from you, Jeff. Go find a job where you are going to learn. The goal isn't to make a huge income from your job. The goal is to make the connections, have the resources, and build the knowledge base ahead of time so that when you do make the jump, you can make it work.

"In general, if anyone is in a situation where they're not happy with what they're doing, then get out and go do something else. Have the courage to do that. For example, if you are in a university class because your parents want you to be a doctor, you need to ask yourself: Are you living your parents' life or are you living your life? A lot of people like to blame others, but it's your life. At what point are you going to cut the cord and say, *I'm an adult and I'm making my own decisions*? Stop blaming others, take the personal accountability and responsibility, and make the change. Do you want to be happy? Then make the change."

Are You as Good as You Think You Are?

"I go to a lot of networking events, and I know a lot of entrepreneurs and friends," I said, "who are putting out lots of content but not growing their YouTube channel the way they'd like. Being that you are one of the top YouTubers in the world, how did you get to where you are today? How did you get from Evan at point zero to as successful as you are today?"

"I've done 3,600 public videos and another 1,000 private videos. You'd have to be really slow to not learn something after doing all those videos. Practicing is important, and quantity leads to quality. Be prolific. You speak, Jeff. I'm sure you're much better at speaking now than you were when you did your first or second speech. Every time you speak you get better. If you speak 100 times a year, you're going to get really good. If you speak two times a year, don't expect to get amazing at it.

"If I look at where I am now," Evan continued, "in both a good and a bad way, I deserve to be where I am. In a good way, my channel has many millions of views. I deserve that because I provided good quality and value to my audience. On the other hand, you say I'm one of the largest YouTubers on the planet – I have half a million subscribers, which is big in the entrepreneur space, I guess, but relative to who's out there, I'm still a medium-sized fish. *And I deserve that.* I don't deserve to be more. My content needs to get better. I need to get better. The editing needs to get better. Everything needs to get better for me to get to where I want to go. If I put out a video and someone doesn't instantly share it, or they don't leave a comment, then I didn't do a good enough job to impact them that day.

"As I get better, I reach a greater percentage of the population, with more people sharing. But I don't deserve more success because I'm not good enough. A lot of people will say, *My content is really good.* Well listen – you had 50 people watch it. How many of them shared it? Did they go home and tell their friends, *You need to watch this video, it's crazy!* No, they didn't. For a lot of people, their content isn't good enough yet, and they need to work on getting better.

"In a market like YouTube, and on all the social platforms, the talent will rise. No one is holding you back. We're not in the early days of NBC and the TV networks when you needed to get through the gatekeeper. For example, if you want to write a book, you don't need Penguin Random House to say, *Yeah, we pick you.* Just publish it. If it's a good book, people will read it, share it, and it'll take off. There are no gatekeepers anymore. It's on all of us to work harder and get better. I need to get better.

If I want to have the impact I feel I can have, I need to work harder. My point here is that I deserve all the success I've had, but I also deserve the lack of success, because I need to work harder and get better."

Before we move on to the next section, let's take a quick pause here. Evan is giving us a lot of valuable insights, all of them practical. Let me point out something incredibly powerful going on right here: I'm talking to an enormously successful individual, someone who casually has YouTube hangout sessions with legends like Brian Tracy. Evan could easily think he's better and above others, but he doesn't. He's humble and always looking to get better. A common theme throughout our conversation is his emphasis on the importance of personal responsibility, and not getting ahead of yourself. This is a common thread with genuinely successful, authentic leaders – they fully believe in themselves and at the same time are grounded enough, in reality, to know that they can do and be more.

Also, keep in mind that Evan is not saying you are not good enough; he's saying your content may not be good enough. You are fully worthy as a person, and you aren't at all to blame for a generally unhappy person who sees your awesome content and criticizes it for no reason. He's saying to keep the focus on what you have control over by staying humble and remembering your skills can always improve.

Start Your Business for the Right Reasons

"I give you a lot of credit," I said. "Here you are talking about how you need to get better and keep growing, yet there are so many people out there who get complacent. And if that's what they want, that's great. At the same time, I give you a lot of credit for saying you need to grow.

Given where you are right now, it would be easy to not have that mindset. You have a winner's mindset.

"Let's say someone wants to get from point A to B as an entrepreneur, and there are landmines everywhere. What would you say are the biggest landmines where entrepreneurs may get stuck?"

"It's important that people have equal parts humbleness and confidence," Evan said. "I feel like I'm not playing at the same level as Tony Robbins and Les Brown. I'm not as good of a speaker as they are and I'm not able to impact people as quickly as they can. But I also don't think I'm bad. I think I'm really good; I'm just not *there* yet. There are people who are ahead of me. A lot of people don't have the balance. They either think they're great and don't do anything to get better, instead choosing to complain about why they don't get more customers or views. Or the opposite is that they're too humble and they never think they're good enough, so they never charge enough or get the results they want because they're too humble. So the mindset of being both humble and confident is important.

"As far as entrepreneurship, a lot of people start their business for the wrong reasons. They are chasing the money, the opportunity, but they forget about the passion. They aren't doing it for the right reasons. The number one trait you'll find in not only any successful entrepreneur but also any successful person, in general, is the passion for what they're doing. It comes down to doing what you do for the right reasons. Money is important – your business is not a charity, and you're not doing this for free – but money is number two. There has to be a greater reason than money. If money is your number one reason for doing something, then you're in the wrong thing. You'll fail. You might have a little bit of success, but you'll never hit what you could hit.

"The other thing is to keep trying by running experiments and running tests. So many people get caught up in their own heads about waiting and having to be perfect, and they never actually do anything. Then someone else goes out there and makes tons of money off of your idea, and you blame that guy, but it's your fault! You had the idea but didn't do anything about it. Take action. Start small. You don't need as much equipment as you think you do. Just start. You want to make a YouTube video? Take out your phone, hit record, start, and make your first video.

"I lost a forty-million dollar deal because of this with my first company. I was so worried about having everything be perfect with the perfect plan that we were too late, and a big company ended up buying our biggest competitor instead of us. I spent way too much time tinkering and not enough time doing. I now don't wait because of the sting of losing a forty-million dollar deal. Hopefully, the people reading this book will learn from this lesson and not have to lose a deal like that themselves. Or maybe you need to go through that rock bottom pain moment to really apply the lesson in your life. What I'm telling you is that if you get an idea, go out and try it. Do it and experiment. Expect it to suck, but keep doing, doing, and doing. Keep growing. This is *much* better than having all these ideas but never doing anything about them."

There's No Need to Jump Off the Cliff

"I'm wondering, how do you balance enjoying today with also being responsible, frugal, and smart with your money?" I asked Evan.

"Even if you don't have the budget to do bigger things," Evan said, "you can still make time for what's important. With my first business, when I had little to no money, my business partners and I would still make time for what mattered. We would celebrate a win when we got a new client. We would celebrate it by going to McDonald's and getting French fries – and the three of us would share the fries.

"With where I'm at today, I might celebrate a little differently because I have more resources – for one of my businesses, every quarter we do something fun. Coming up we have a day of snow tubing and then dinner, and I can pay for that. The idea of celebration is the same concept regardless of the resources you have. It started with McDonald's French fries and now has evolved into something bigger, but the idea is the same.

"When my book was published, and we saw it in the bookstore, I celebrated with my wife by going to McDonald's and getting French fries. Even now, I still associate those fries with victory because I ingrained that into myself. Over time your financial flexibility will improve, but the concepts stay the same. If you're an entrepreneur and you're trying to get something off the ground, I wouldn't go all-in. I'm not the guy who says to put a flame-thrower to your boss's office and burn every bridge you have, making it a forced decision. I like the planning – I'm much more risk-averse as an entrepreneur than most people think you have to be. You don't have to be a crazy, risk-loving person to have success in business."

"I love what you just said there," I said to Evan. "Some people will tell you to jump off the cliff and grow wings on the way down. I tried that twice in the past, and it didn't work for me. I wasn't foolish or reckless or anything like that, but on several occasions I dove head-first into entrepreneurship before I had systems in place and before I really knew what I was doing. I was gung-ho and all-in, and to my credit, I genuinely worked my butt off, did my best, and made progress. But it just wasn't happening and didn't bring in enough sustainable income to do it full-time. It wasn't the end of the world, and I was able to get through it by taking on jobs, but I learned from the experience that it's not about putting your finances into reckless endangerment to make your dreams come true. It's about building a bridge while you have income and taking it one step at a time. That's why I love your practical approach to the entrepreneurial process. When I hear someone on a YouTube video telling their audience to go all-in right now, I don't always agree with it. It sounds great in a motivational video but isn't always reality. I'm not saying it can't happen, and if or when someone pulls it off, I genuinely applaud them. I'm just saying it's a lot harder than one may initially think or realize. I learned that the hard way."

"Exactly; I'd ease my way into it," Evan said. "Again, I'd try to find a job where I'm making a paycheck, and I'm learning, picking up valuable experience. If you want to be a real estate agent, you don't get there by working as an accountant. You get there by going and working for a real estate company, and seeing if you can improve yourself.

You get there by doing real estate on the side. Try to get your own real estate business going. Start to get some friends and family to invest in a fund that would allow you to buy a house.

"When it gets to the point where your side hustle is bringing in enough income to support you full-time, then you can think about making the leap. I'm not talking about luxury. I'm not talking about buying a Lamborghini or anything. I'm just talking about making enough to support you at a basic level, like paying for a place to live, food, and Internet. Also, you want to be at a point where you feel like you've learned enough from your job. *Then* go full-time on your business. Some people have different thresholds as far as what their standard of living needs to be, but that transition is what would be best to do for someone who is starting out now, especially if you have a mortgage and kids.

"Some people need to go all-in because that's the only way they get committed, so if that's your personality type then think about that option, but otherwise plan a much safer approach."

Ego or No Ego?

"This is great stuff, Evan," I said. "There's one school of thought out there that is totally against ego. And there's another school of thought out there that says it's good to use ego to your advantage, that it can benefit you. I know you talked earlier about having a balance between humbleness and confidence. Is there a balancing point between those two schools of thought which seem to contradict each other? Some say you need ego to be successful, and others say if you have ego you'll come across as arrogant."

"Sure there is," Evan said. "For a lot of these things, we default to one side, but you gain a lot of personal power and impact by learning more about the other side. For example, someone who is super-humble and has zero ego has a visceral reaction to anyone who has any ego. Those kinds of people can't deal with ego at all. They then get concerned that if they get a little bit of ego, they are going to fall off the deep end and become an egomaniac.

"Here's the thing: That person will never become an egomaniac. It's never going to happen. They get so concerned with becoming an egomaniac that they make it a point to stay where they are. They are so humble – from their upbringing – that they could use a little bit more ego and confidence to help them. But they're never going to fall off the deep end.

"And you'll find this dichotomy everywhere, not just in business but in life. You get some people who only want to plan, plan, and do more planning. They need everything to be perfect, and they never take any action. Then you have people who constantly take action, but never plan; they just fly by the seat of their pants. Neither is good! You need a combination. The planner needs to act more, and the person taking action needs to plan more. You're never going to go off to the other side. The over-planner is never going to not care about planning again and just go crazy in taking action; this is what they're concerned about. They're concerned they are going to lose their core to go chase this crazy thing. The solution is to move a little bit closer to the middle. You may not ever get there, but move a little bit closer to the middle because you're still going to keep your core. But at the same time, the skills you're going to learn and the mindset you'll gain with that better approach will help you go off and accomplish exactly what it is you're looking to accomplish.

"The key to remember here is that you can learn from the other side without having to go off the deep end."

I asked Evan this question because I had a friend (who, for the record, is a great guy) who criticized me for showing a little bit of confidence at a networking event. He said I wasn't being humble enough. My whole life I've been overly humble, and after a long, transformative process, I'm now finally integrating the other side into my actions. Low and behold, someone who is purely humble didn't like that. He falls into the camp of viscerally reacting negatively to anyone who shows even the slightest bit of ego. I'm glad Evan cleared this up for me – his negative reaction to me was more a reflection of his own internal workings than it was of me. I share this with you so that when someone criticizes you for finding that balance, you can let it go in one ear and out the other.

Parting Shots

"Evan, do you have any parting shots for someone who is struggling right now, someone who is in the trenches and pushing daily, yet also struggling? What do you have for them?"

"Just believe," Evan said. "Believe in what you're doing. Believe it's going to work out. Believe in the project. This is going to be the hardest thing you ever do in your life. You're going to have tons of roadblocks along the way, and that's why you're going to have to love what you're doing so much – because you're crazy. A normal, rational, sane person would quit, give up, and go do something logical and safe. Accept that: It's normal, failure is part of the process, and if you have a deep passion for doing it then just continue on. Believe. Don't quit too soon and then regret that decision for the rest of your life."

"Your insights are so powerful, Evan," I said. "I definitely appreciate the discussion, and I'm looking forward to featuring you in my book."

"Thanks for the great questions, Jeff," Evan said. "I'm sure you'll hit me up when this book is done. Good luck with the writing process."

Chapter 9: Cut the Cord and Set Yourself Free

Go "all in" or get "all out."
There's nothing worse than living life halfhearted.
– Rebekah Radice

My face-to-face meeting with Steve Scott happened on St. Patrick's Day, Friday, March 17th, 2017, at a Starbucks in Paramus, New Jersey. He's a successful author and entrepreneur, his content is excellent, and he's an all-around awesome guy.

Go All-In

"You've achieved a high level of success as an author," I said to Steve. "Tell me more about your story and how you got to where you are."

"I was in the military from 1999 to 2001," Steve said. "I was frequently on guard duty, and I had absolutely no control over my schedule. I would literally be thrown in jail if I quit, and I didn't like the lack of freedom. After the military, I worked a 9-to-5 job. The job was okay, but I didn't like the lack of freedom there either. It was the desire for freedom that got me started on my entrepreneurial journey.

"From 2003 to 2005 I made a lot of dumb mistakes, and my business went nowhere. In 2006 I realized that if I really wanted control of my life, I was going to have to get to know the ropes of business much better. That's when I really got serious."

"At what point did you start doing your business full-time, stepping away from the job you had?" I asked. "And how did you fund your ventures; did you save a lot of money while working?"

"In 2005 I took the plunge," Steve said. "I used credit cards to fund it. I don't recommend others doing this, but it did fund my ventures while I was getting started. I was focusing on affiliate marketing."

"I used credit cards to fund a lot of my initial costs as well," I said.

"Yeah, I'm out of debt now, and I've been out of debt for many years," Steve said. "But it did help me get off the ground."

Before we move further, let me share with you something important: Although credit cards did work for Steve and me, please use them at your own discretion. We are NOT suggesting for you to go into credit card debt; we are simply being transparent and open about our journeys. Credit card debt is dangerous and can be difficult to get out of, so our recommendation to you is to be smarter than Steve and me by doing your best to pay for things with cash and be careful with every expenditure. Credit cards are useful as a last resort option when you need to eat (or something of that sort), but focus on staying debt-free as much as possible. If you choose to go into debt, make sure it's a calculated and well-planned risk.

This may mean that instead of diving blindly and head first into a venture, you grow it slowly while you have other income (as Evan talked about in the previous chapter). Achieving success is not about being reckless and impulsive, but rather smart and strategic.

"You talked about really not liking the lack of freedom," I said to Steve, "and I know many feel the same way. You also mentioned getting really serious about learning the ins and outs of business. I'm wondering, in addition to this, did you have a specific turning point or was it more a general process over time?"

"Yeah, my turning point was when I got out of a terrible relationship," Steve said, "and I went to Europe to travel. The businesses I had up to that point were okay, but I didn't put my all into them; I didn't go all-in. While traveling Europe, I made a promise to myself. This was one of those promises you 100% keep no matter what. I promised myself that with the next good business opportunity that arises, I'd go all-in. In the past, I had good ideas but never pursued them fully. For example, I dumped an email list I had created. I also got rid of several businesses that had potential to turn into big things, but I didn't stick with them. I was always pushing off businesses.

"When I got back from Europe, a new business opportunity did arise. I remembered the promise I made to myself and this time I ran with it. I went all-in – and I became successful doing it."

This is huge and a core realization of creating prosperity for yourself through authenticity: Stop making half-hearted attempts at your business, your relationships, and your life. Go all-in. When you make the inner decision to go all-in, you automatically increase your chances of succeeding by allowing yourself to tap into the core of who you are. Your innate genius and authenticity emerge when you truly go *all-in*.

Stop Giving a F*ck What People Think

"You are an authentic guy," I said. "What is the key to taking off the mask and truly being yourself in a world that is constantly trying to get us to be like someone else?"

"First, it's having and developing faith in your own intuition," Steve said. "Second, it's finding happiness within yourself, not the outside world. Third, it's not giving a fuck what other people think."

I laughed.

"Love it," I said. "Can I write it in the book exactly as you said it just now?"

"Yes," Steve said. "There's really no better way to put it. I'm in my forties now, and I really don't care what other people think. When I was your age, in my late twenties and early thirties, I did care what other people thought. But not anymore. I drive a crappy, beat-up car. I enjoy spending time with people I care about. And I don't need to buy the latest iPhone."

Steve's authenticity really shines through here, and what he said is so powerful it bears reiterating: **he values people over things; he's not obsessed with having to have the latest gadgets and technological advances; and he's transparent, freely admitting that he truly doesn't care what other people think.**

I can relate to Steve in deciding to not care about people's thoughts and judgments. For the longest time after college, I was trying to gain the approval of people who didn't accept me during that period of my life. I had friends in college, but I was focused on winning over the people who didn't like me. I would do epic things – for example, I went to Kuala Lumpur, Malaysia, to compete in the semifinals of the World Championship of Public Speaking, and also I published my first book through a publisher – and I thought, *Now I've earned the approval of my college classmates. Now I can be happy because they'll finally accept me.* That's when I went to a college reunion in New York City where some of the people in the same graduating class as me were in attendance.

Some of them disrespected me by ignoring me, not talking to me, and otherwise dismissing me. The event wasn't a total disaster, as I did make some great connections at the event, but at the end of the day I felt left out and isolated, a feeling I hadn't experienced in many years. This was the same thing they did to me in college, and they were still doing it, despite the progress I had made in my business and life. No hard feelings here, and I'm only sharing this for your benefit, but I left that event genuinely frustrated. After I had time to reflect on the experience, I decided to completely, 100%, stop living my life to gain the acceptance of others, especially my judgmental college classmates. This was a turning point for me, as I decided to cut the cord that tied my happiness to their acceptance of me. And I've never felt freer (this is coming from someone who was tied to the chains of what other people thought all four years of high school, all four years of college, and many years out of college). Ironically, I'm now in a position to most effectively help and serve others.

When you cut the cord that ties your happiness to the need to be accepted by others, you most effectively position yourself as someone who can help others.

This is what Steve means when he says that he no longer cares what other people think. You'll never meet a guy more ready and willing to help other people, yet the very reason he's able to do this so effectively is that he's not worried about other people accepting him or not. Instead, he's focused on how he can make a real impact on the world. The catch-22 is that freeing yourself from caring about how people perceive you is what will allow your innate authenticity to really shine through.

"I just got back from a conference in California," Steve continued, "and I got a chance to see Pat Flynn speak. I also spoke with him. Pat is the kind of person I gravitate towards – someone who enjoys being themselves. I don't like the kind of person who will put on airs, being someone they're not.

"Also, while we're still on this topic, I want to point out that I do care when I get a negative review from someone on one of my books," Steve said. "I care in the sense that I want to make sure my work is high quality and really helping other people."

Although Steve has definitely evolved beyond letting other people's opinions throw him off his game or make him change course, he does care what people think in the sense that he wants to make sure he's adding value to people and delivering what he said he'll deliver. Not caring what other people think does *not* mean you become oblivious to feedback, reviews, and other aspects of constructive criticism that may be worth hearing. As we discussed earlier in the book, getting feedback from the right kinds of people is crucial to your success. The trick is to learn to tune out the majority of irrelevant comments, instead tuning into the few comments that do matter. Continue to disregard the many ignorant comments that mean absolutely nothing, but don't forget to take note of the specific feedback that can help you get to your next level.

Play Your Own Game

"What advice do you have for someone who is just starting out?" I asked. "And when I say 'just starting out,' this goes for anyone at the beginning of their career, whatever their chosen career path may be."

"Your life doesn't have to mean working a crazy number of hours," Steve said, "like some people say you have to do. It took me a long time to learn that I'm happy when I work for a reasonable number of hours each day, without going crazy. If I write for at least a couple of hours in a day, I'm good."

This is coming from a professional writer, someone who literally writes books for a living. Steve is the epitome of redefining what success means, which was the core theme of my previous book *Reach Your Mountaintop*. It's your life, not anyone else's, and it's up to you to decide what's best for your schedule. A lot of people get brainwashed with the idea that they have to pull crazy, insane hours to be successful. Yes, that's sometimes required, but it's not usually necessary. Slow and steady wins the race. I'm all for making that big push, but I'm also all for knowing your limits and keeping your schedule in balance.

I realize Steve has become successful enough to afford himself the lifestyle where he's able to write for a few hours, do a few other important tasks, and then call it a day, but how often are the binds we place on ourselves self-imposed? Here are a few quick examples you might relate to; I've been guilty of these as much as anyone else:

- We stay late at work to please our boss, even though many of our coworkers leave earlier.

- We spend our entire weekend working nonstop, even though every ounce of our being is screaming at us to stop and take a break.
- We endlessly compare ourselves to other people, never feeling good enough and never celebrating our achievements the way we deserve.

The point here is to play your own game and run your own race. Know that you don't need to copy someone else to be successful; you can create your own formula for success. Yes, it's perfectly okay to follow thought leaders out there, but don't let their formula interfere with what you know is right for you.

"This is powerful," I said to Steve, "and it makes a lot of sense. I know of several speakers and authors out there, who I'll respectfully leave unnamed, who are crazy about the need to work insane hours. And please don't get me wrong, these guys are super-successful and have earned their right to share their wisdom. I'm not criticizing or condemning them in any way whatsoever; I'm all for hard work. What I'm saying is that I've done the fifteen-hour workdays, and I've worked entire weekends nonstop, and it simply doesn't work for me. I wake up on Monday after these crazy weekends, and I'm miserable. I'm a happy person, so I know when I'm feeling miserable I'm not doing something right."

"I agree," Steve said. "It's about learning to be happy paying the bills. I have a 'monthly nut' that covers my bills and necessities, and if I hit it, I'm happy. One month I'll make $65,000, and another month I'll make $10,000. It's about being happy with what you have. I don't need more. Some people are in the trap of needing more.

"Also, some people have a down month, and they think of it as a reflection of themselves. It's not though. A down month is not a reflection of your worth."

If you have a down month in business or some other aspect of your life, by all means, figure out what needs to change and what you need to do differently to get back on your high horse. But remember that your business and your level of wealth are not a factor in your self-worth.

"You just hit the nail on the head," I said to Steve. "One of my core messages, when I speak, is that your self-worth does not depend on external circumstances. And that's exactly what you're saying here. A down month is not a reflection of your worth as a person. Yes, it may indicate a need for a tweak in your day-to-day operations. But it also may be a reflection of the fact that there are flat-out ups and downs in business, such as seasonal factors outside of your control."

"Well put," Steve said. "It's also important to celebrate your success. Are you improving? Are you making progress? You need to support yourself along the way. Ask yourself: *What works for me?* And establish daily habits. If you want to write a book, then write every day. I try to write for at least a minimum of thirty minutes each day. Some days I'm able to write for two hours or more, but even on an off-day, I write too. Consistency is better than feast or famine."

"This has been awesome, Steve," I said. "I'm looking forward to featuring you in the book. What you said here today ties into the core message of it, and ties nicely into what the other experts said as well."

Chapter 10: Rewire Yourself

"Chains of habit are too light to be felt
until they are too heavy to be broken."
– Warren Buffett

Limit Your Distractions and Really Focus

I spoke with entrepreneur and search engine optimization (SEO) expert Rick Cleri over lunch while eating some delicious sushi. He has achieved an enormous amount of entrepreneurial success, and I wanted to pick his brain further about some of his insights.

"What's the key to really getting ahead in business and life?" I asked.

"Less is more," Rick said. "Do fewer things, but do those fewer things better. People often have a lot going on, managing countless priorities. And I get it because I used to be that way. But what I've found to be the key to really getting ahead is zeroing in on those few key priorities and tasks. Pick your biggest goal and focus on it. The rest will come later."

"That makes sense," I said. "I'm much more focused than I used to be, but I still find myself juggling competing priorities. It's tough."

"Say no," Rick said. "You owe it to yourself to do that. Say no to enough things so that you free up the time, space, and energy to do what you really want to do."

"This is great," I said. "What would you say is the key to authenticity?"

"Being present and in the moment with the people you're with," Rick said. "If you notice, I put my phone face down on the side of this table, and I'm not going to check it until this lunch is over. People are calling me and texting me right now, but I'm not going to let that distraction take away from our lunch."

I looked and saw Rick's phone face down on the table.

"A lot of people are lost in endless distraction," Rick said. "They're never present and really with you in the moment. When I'm with someone, I make sure to be there 100%, and not on my phone."

If you are not present and in the moment, you will limit your ability to be authentic. Genuine connections happen when you stop endlessly checking your phone, instead choosing to focus on the person or people you're with.

There's a time and place to check email and social media, as they are useful tools. But when you are with other people, that is *not* the time to check your notifications unless it's an emergency. But more often than not, it's not emergency – we check our phones out of habit or addiction.

Here's an exercise that's worked well for me, and perhaps it will also work well for you: Take a break from social media. As I write these words, I just completed a hiatus from social media that lasted for more than 100 days. I forced myself to do this because for the longest time, I was addictively checking my social media accounts multiple times each day and it was limiting my productivity, impact, and success. The first couple of weeks off of social media were extremely difficult, but it got easier as time went on.

For the record, social media has a lot of positive uses and functions. It only became negative for me when I lost the balance and checked it too frequently. The same goes for email: I didn't take a 100-day hiatus from email as that wouldn't have made sense for my business, but I did reduce the number of times I check it. Also, I no longer check email first thing in the morning – I now usually wait until the afternoon to check it. I advise you do the same. What I am encouraging you to do is take a break from social media. It definitely doesn't have to be as extreme as my more-than-100-day hiatus, but try a week off, or even a couple days. If you're really hooked on it, start with staying off it for one day. You might find it harder than you initially expected, but you'll thank yourself when your productivity increases.

Shatter Your Limiting Beliefs

I first met entrepreneur and speaker Kevin Laylor at the Fall 2016 District 18 Toastmasters Conference in Maryland. Although I now live in Connecticut, I still go down to Maryland for District 18 Toastmasters Conferences because I have a large number of friends who are part of that group. After I graduated college, I lived in Baltimore for many years and made some amazing connections through Toastmasters and other organizations. I stayed in touch with many of these awesome, life-changing connections, and I enjoy seeing them throughout each year.

My heart-to-heart conversation with Kevin Laylor came at the perfect time for me. I was experiencing some challenges with my business and his inspiration and wisdom really spoke to me. It's my hope that his words will speak to you as well.

"A lot of people walk around with limiting beliefs," Kevin said. "I'm here to tell you that you can get rid of those limiting beliefs. For example, a lot of people claim to never have the time or money to start their own business. But they continue spending money on things they don't really need. If you're really serious about growing your business, move somewhere cheaper that costs you less. People have the belief that they need their apartment or home to be a certain size, but that's limiting them."

This is incredibly powerful. What Kevin is talking about is not buying into society's belief system – the idea that you need to *appear* wealthy and successful to the outside world. Remember what Steve Scott said in the previous chapter? He's wealthy, but he chooses to drive a beat-up car because he doesn't care what other people think. Kevin is talking about the same thing. Don't let the false belief that your worth as a person depends on how other people perceive you get in your way. Don't let the limiting belief of needing to look cool to your friends stop you from doing the work you are really meant to do.

Apply Kevin's wisdom and shatter your limiting beliefs. Get smart about your finances and adjust your living situation to accommodate your dream. If you are in your twenties and have at least a decent relationship with your parents, move back home. If you are in your thirties living on your own, consider downsizing or getting roommates. Sell your home if you have to. There are always options.

You might be thinking right now, *This is great and I agree, but how do I go about shattering my limiting beliefs?* I'm glad you asked. There are a few simple steps you can use to shatter your limiting beliefs, and you need to make sure you repeat these steps over time.

First, on a recording device of some sort like a camcorder, record yourself saying your new belief. Have classical music playing in the background while doing the recording, which will further ingrain your new beliefs into your subconscious mind. Then upload the recording to your computer and/or iPod and play it back to yourself several times a week, or whenever you get a chance during a given month.

What I'll do is go on the Internet and find a hypnotic induction script of some kind, which allows me to fully relax when listening to it. That way when I do get to the suggestion/affirmation/new belief, my subconscious mind is ready to receive it. The first part of the recording is the hypnotic induction, and the second part is the new belief(s). Here are some suggested new beliefs to program into your mind through this process:

- I am worthy exactly as I am. My self-worth is independent of the external world.
- I create, attract, and maintain wealth. I do not need to appear wealthy to the outside world, knowing my true wealth is on the inside. My debts steadily decrease, and I spend my money responsibly.
- I lose weight. My weight loss happens naturally and easily. I am my ideal weight.
- I am confident and attractive. I am a Divine expression of life.
- I earn money living my dreams. I am a [your dream career/profession].

You get the picture. You are only limited by your own creativity (shout-out to my friend Stuart Pink, an author and speaker, who talks about the importance of creativity and how to be more creative). I started doing these meditative scripts while I was in high school and college playing sports, and I've used them for everything from mastering social situations and losing weight, to becoming a paid professional speaker and bestselling author. Like anything else, this takes time, repetition, and practice. I realize this isn't the sexy, quick-fix solution most of society wants, but real change takes time and effort. If it were easy, everyone would do it – that's why so many people walk around their entire lives with limiting beliefs. But you're not one of them.

Note: Earlier in this book, entrepreneur Suzanne Duret talked with us about not going overboard with vision boards and visualization. This section does not in any way contradict Suzanne's insights – here, we are talking more about rewiring your internal workings more than we are talking about the need to obsess over achieving a particular result or exact goal. Yes, the process outlined here can be used for external goals, but the focus is on your internal beliefs. You only need to do this once a day, a few times a week, or even once a week/month. The point here is to give you a simple, practical process that will allow you to rewire your subconscious mind for the better, while you continue to take continuous action. When I say this process takes time, I'm referring to it as something you want to keep doing over many weeks and months, but keep in mind that the total amount of time you need to dedicate to the process each particular week is small.

Another tactic that has worked for a lot of people is to record your negative thoughts in a journal at the end of each day. You'd be amazed how often you will find yourself focusing on something negative. What this process allows you to do is to become aware of your negative thoughts so you can change and replace them. Don't try to fight your negative thoughts; instead, become the alert witness and observer to your thought patterns and choose to replace negative thoughts with positive ones.

Finally, write down a positive affirmation on a notecard and carry it with you in your wallet or purse. Show yourself the notecard affirmation several times a day. Consciously repeat the affirmation in your mind throughout the day, like on your lunch break and when you are in the bathroom. This may seem silly or inconsequential, but you'd be amazed at the power we hold in our conscious minds to shape and craft the way we think, feel, and act.

Leaders work on actively improving their limiting beliefs.

What You Focus on Expands

You've probably been hearing from people your whole life (starting with teachers in kindergarten and elementary school) that you need to focus on the positive. But, I know life isn't always a positive and warm place (look at what happened, for example, to my mom's students at Sandy Hook Elementary, my old elementary school). With that said, it's important to know that *what you focus on expands.*

This book is about the power of authentic leadership, so I want to take you into a big mistake I've consistently made: I frequently focus on the negative instead of the positive. I was in New York City hanging out with my good friend Ashir Nelson, an entrepreneur and LinkedIn expert. I was telling him how it bothers me that all successful authors have some amount of negative reviews on Amazon.

"You're focused on the wrong thing," Ashir said to me. "You're focused on the negative. These authors you are talking about are also making a huge difference in the lives of countless people. Stop focusing on the small amount of negative reviews they have and start focusing on the large amount of positive reviews they have.

"Let's take all the people you've ever known. If you put into one group the people who like and support you, and you put into another group the people who really don't like you, I guarantee the group of supporters will be MUCH bigger than the group of people who don't like you."

"You're absolutely right," I said to Ashir.

My little brother Jamie also helped me to shift past the negative, and I hope he'll help you do the same. In 2015 I did a TEDx talk, and I got a lot of great feedback about the talk. But there were a few people who didn't like it, as well as a couple of haters on YouTube. The people who liked my TEDx, *How to Fulfill Your Inner Life,* FAR outweighed the people who didn't like it, yet I found myself feeling down and upset about the people who didn't like it.

In a moment of weakness, I shared my thoughts with my wise little brother, Jamie, and he responded with compassion.

"Jeff," Jamie said, "it's ridiculous to be focusing on a couple of people who didn't like your talk. You did great, and a lot of people liked it. That's what matters. You can never please everybody."

This was really powerful advice, and it's why I frequently find myself going to my little brother for advice.

My TEDx talk gave me added exposure to people in the world, and with added exposure comes critics. I wasn't used to thousands of people watching one of my videos, and I was caught off guard by some of the trolls on YouTube. But Ashir and Jamie helped me out of that mindset by reminding me that I could change my habituated ways of thinking. At the time of writing this, my TEDx talk has 71 up votes and only 2 down votes. With Jamie's help, I was able to stop worrying about those 2 down votes and instead focus on those 71 up votes. The talk made a difference in people's lives, and that's what counts.

Remind yourself as often as you reasonably can that what you focus on expands, and the positive far outweighs the negative.

Chapter 11: Screw It

Powerful Insights From a New York Times Bestselling Author

As part of an interview for this book, I was able to pick the mind of leadership, time management, and employee engagement expert Kevin Kruse. His insights tie right into the message of this book.

"What is the secret to being authentic in a world that is trying to get us to be like everyone else?" I asked Kevin.

"It's very tough," Kevin said. "Most people are walking the tightrope between their need to express their own identity and their need to fit in. These are really primal urges. For me, I remind myself daily of all the things I'm grateful for in life, and that I only really need the love and approval of my kids and a couple of close friends to be happy. When you don't NEED to be liked or loved by everyone, it frees you up to be your true self."

"That's a great point, and it's something that we all struggle with," I said. "What are some tips and tactics you have to stay true to yourself and follow your own inner compass even when other people are not agreeing with what you're doing?"

"It helps to be really clear about your own values and goals," Kevin said. "If you know what you are trying to achieve and what you will and won't do to achieve it, it becomes easier to ignore the naysayers."

"Yes," I said. "Knowing your core values is crucial. In the beginning of your book, *15 Secrets Successful People Know About Time Management,* you shared how you used to overwork yourself, drinking red bulls and pulling crazy hours. This was a great story and relatable for a lot of people. What are your thoughts in general on people revealing their mistakes and flaws for the benefit of other people to learn from them?"

"The reason why authenticity is so powerful," Kevin said, "is that it accelerates trust. Who normally tells us about their failures, their most embarrassing moments, and the times they were scared? Usually, it's family members or our closest friends. So when a boss at work, or a sales person, or a new date very quickly shares their 'weakest' moments, it triggers feelings of familial closeness. We automatically trust the person more and are thankful they would share with us at a personal level."

"Love it," I said. "This has been the big secret behind my ability to connect with people from the stage. I'm more vulnerable than the audience initially expects me to be, and it establishes a genuine connection. I'd also like to point out that some people get going with their dreams and make initial progress but can't seem to fully break free from the restraints, obligations, and expectations of friends and family who want them to choose a certain career path or make a particular decision. Do you have advice for someone who is making good initial gains, but still facing the daily struggle of dealing with people who don't believe in their dreams? For example, dealing with unavoidable people such as family and coworkers."

"It's harsh, but in the movie, *Boiler Room*, Jim Young, played by Ben Affleck, says, 'Fuck them! Fuck'em! Parents don't like the life you lead? Fuck you, Mom and Dad. See how it feels when you're making their fucking Lexus payments.'

"It's natural for parents and others to want to protect you, but they can only give you advice and judge you based on their own life filter. That's fine. You need to be true to yourself. YOU are the one that will be sitting in a rocking chair at age 85 thinking back on YOUR life. What do you need to do today to make sure you have no regrets?"

"That's incredibly powerful Kevin," I said. "Last question. What are some ways an individual could get to know themselves better?"

"Take a bunch of personality profiles like Myers-Briggs, Disc, or StrengthsFinder. Get a coach."

Sometimes you just have to say screw it by forgetting the haters and doing you.

Chapter 12: It's Not Always Easy, but You'll Thank Yourself

"Always do what's right; this will gratify some and astonish the rest."
– Albert Einstein

I had a chance to interview successful author Nick Thacker for this book, someone whom I communicated with in the past and featured in-depth in my previous book *Reach Your Mountaintop*. His insights are perfect for us as we head into the final chapters of this book – they cover the sentiment of what we've already discussed, add new insights, and are the ideal preparation for the ending of this book.

Some of the questions I asked Nick are similar to the questions I asked other experts, but the beauty is we get to hear another perspective. Nick is a genius and has a lot to offer us. His level of authenticity is through the roof, and he's a fantastic living example of the long-term benefit of being authentic.

It's Not Always Easy to Be Authentic, But Do It Anyway

"What is the secret to being authentic in a world that is trying to get us to be like everyone else?" I asked Nick.

"I love this question," Nick said, "because of the implication. I hope everyone can agree that authenticity is a FAR better long-term strategy than a lack of transparency. There's really no 'secret,' either. Often it comes down to a simple question: Is what I'm about to do/say/think the easy way out? If so, it's probably not authentic.

"Of course this needs some clarification because not EVERYTHING that's easiest is wrong or bad or inauthentic. It's just that the times when our career capital will benefit most by being authentic, it's usually easiest to NOT be authentic. Tell the truth and be real, even if it hurts you. If it hurts someone else, do it tactfully, privately, and out of a place of respect and support. If you can't do that, don't do anything – move on."

"When you say 'It's just that the times when our career capital will benefit most by being authentic, it's usually easiest to not be authentic'," I asked, "are you saying that when our careers will benefit from being authentic, we are not authentic because it's easier to do so? And we don't realize that being authentic would have been a better choice because it didn't feel like it at the moment? I'm making up this example off the top of my head: Let's say someone is working a job on a project. And let's hypothetically say they despise the project and are barely making any progress on it. When they sit down with their boss for an update, it would be easiest to sugarcoat the update and make themselves look good. But it might be better for them to be transparent and authentic by saying something like, *Look, this project is not going well, I'm struggling with it, etc.* Upon hearing that, a reasonable boss might give them help, reassign them to a different project, or give them a different job altogether. But none of those benefits would have occurred if the person doing the tough project wasn't authentic and transparent. Is this example a good demonstration of what you mean by that?"

"Exactly like that," Nick said. "Think about the possible outcomes of that situation: A reasonable boss would understand, and you'd either get reassigned, given more/different resources, or told to suck it up with a promise that the next project will be amazing. Or if you have an unreasonable boss: You do the hard thing and tell him the truth, and he might fire you. In which case I have to believe that outcome was just a matter of time – you were never going to be really happy there with that sort of unreasonable 'leadership,' and you and your career are going to be better for it down the road.

"Or – and this has been my experience telling the truth and doing the hard thing in exactly this sort of situation – your unreasonable boss might actually surprise you with one of the reasonable boss's responses. Finally, consider what happens when you have a reasonable and competent boss. Your output and results probably speak for themselves, so what are they going to be thinking if you suck up and tell them things are fine, you like the project, etc.?"

It's Okay to Authentically Share Your "Why" With Others

"What are some tips and tactics you use to stay true to yourself and follow your own inner compass even when other people are not agreeing with what you're doing?" I asked Nick.

"Neil Gaiman's commencement speech should be required reading, or – even better – required watching/listening," Nick said. "He talks about 'moving toward your mountain,' and how everything you do professionally either moves you closer to or farther from that mountain. Most of us have no trouble – if we really take some time to process and think about it – knowing what our 'mountain' is, so it's pretty easy to recognize what will move us closer.

"I used to do web design and marketing as a freelancer, as well as my day job and writing. When I became a dad, I knew immediately that freelance was moving me farther from my mountain, because my mountain was having a family and entertaining/inspiring people through writing. Period. It was then just a matter of telling the clients I had and anyone 'in the pipeline' the truth about this, and start moving that work off my plate. Eventually, I stopped doing it altogether, save for helping friends or family. It wasn't easy, but I knew it was what I had to do.

"Best of all? Every time I was authentic and truthful about the 'why' behind this decision, the response was overwhelmingly positive – they all got it right away, and it was no trouble at all moving that type of work to another person or place."

"I've heard some people suggest," I said, "that it's best to never give others an explanation. While there are cases in the 'move on' category that may warrant no explanation, I really resonate with you when you say that it's good to share an authentic and truthful 'why' behind a particular decision. When I'm saying no to someone, or not agreeing to the request, I've also found it beneficial to share a 'why,' especially when the person you are communicating with is someone you like and trust."

"Right!" Nick said. "I've always been a 'why guy,' so I typically project that feeling on others. At the very least, even if they disagree about my reason, they can't deny the fact that their assumed reason is different than my stated one. Maybe that'll hold up in court better.

"The 'never complain, never explain' mantra was I think from Benjamin Disraeli. It's British, so I feel like it must be wise, but it doesn't mean we have to always listen to it either. I don't think I'm very good at never explaining!"

"I'm the same way," I said. "You mentioned Neil Gaiman's commencement speech, and I listened to it. It was one of the best I've ever heard – at the same level as Steve Jobs' commencement speech, as well as J.K. Rowling's and Conan O'Brien's. I had one of those intuitive realizations when Neil said how he struggles to enjoy the journey. I've struggled with that as well. I never really stopped to enjoy all that I did with my second book, the first one I featured you in. I'm hard at work on my third book now. My girlfriend, who is very supportive of all I do, says that I'm overly ambitious, and she's absolutely right. Ambition is an awesome quality to have, but there has to be a time when you stop and have fun. I'll have to make it a point once I publish this third book to consciously stop and enjoy it."

"Yeah, I love the concept of celebrating 'little victories,' " Nick said. "It's as simple as grabbing a slightly more expensive whiskey whenever I get another 100 reviews on a book or treating myself to a nice night out when I hit a milestone. Things like that seem to help calm the nerves about the negative influences in our lives as well.

"I think it was Tim Ferriss who first said he didn't want to be rich, he just wanted to live like the people who were. I love that sentiment – I don't care about having money, but I do want safety, security, and comfort for my family. I don't want to wait until I'm 65-years-old to start enjoying my life!"

Don't Be Afraid to Splurge and Enjoy Life, but Do so Within Reason

"What are a few of your hacks for staying on a budget and building wealth, yet at the same time splurging every once in a while and having fun?" I asked.

"I don't really believe I'll retire," Nick said. "I mean this in principle. Retirement might not be a 'myth,' but it is for me. My family doesn't feel like waiting around for a day when there will be a huge chunk of money waiting for us in an account. We don't want to wait until then to enjoy life. We have kids, friends, are young, and have enough income to do things that are fun.

"Because of those things, we spend money on experiences that we will remember, and we're not afraid to spend a lot – within reason. We won't go into debt for this stuff, and I'll always be focused on saving and bringing in more money, but we're not interested in socking away everything we earn and living frugally for some mysterious time in the future when we'll be able to spend it.

"The practical: We save regularly and automatically, splitting the income into different accounts (retirement, college savings, emergency fund, vehicle, house, etc.). We still have retirement accounts, but I can't imagine a day when I'll just want to sit around and not work on something. We track spending to make sure we're not getting ridiculous in any particular area and pay off credit cards each month.

"In addition, I'm always looking for ways to make life easier or better, like home automation, outsourcing, and things like that. And I'm always looking for ways to earn more. By focusing on these two things, I believe our lives can be spent focusing on the things that are truly important."

When It's Necessary to Make a Change, Have the Guts to Make the Change

"Some people get going with their dreams and make initial progress," I said to Nick, "but can't seem to fully break free from the restraints, obligations, and expectations of friends and family who want them to choose a certain career path or make a particular decision. Any advice for someone who is making good initial gains, but still facing the daily struggle of dealing with people who don't believe in their dreams? This includes dealing with unavoidable people like family and coworkers."

"I hate to say it," Nick said, "but I'm a firm believer in removing negative influences from your life as soon as you recognize them. Have a terrible boss? Quit. Have a friend who's fun to hang out with but always brings you, the world, and everything down? Get a different friend who supports you. Have a family member who doesn't buy into your dreams/goals? Move away.

"This is tricky when it's a spouse, but I'd suggest it's a deeper problem than lack of belief; there are people out there trained to help. For the other instances above, I've dealt with those situations and done exactly what I suggested. It wasn't easy, and it wasn't without pain. But I am FAR better off now without the negative influences in my life, and it turns out there were people I liked even more who also supported my dreams and goals as well. True story – I moved away from my home state, quit a well-paying job, and stopped engaging with old friends. Life continued, and I'm happier than ever for it.

"It helps that I've always been independent, and a bit arrogant. I'm confident in my abilities, but honest about my weaknesses, and I think that has helped me say 'no' to these situations and start actively trying to replace them with better ones."

Parting Shots from Author Nick Thacker

"What are some ways an individual could get to know themselves better?" I asked.

"I love doing the personality profile tests, like Myers-Briggs, Disc, etc.," Nick said. "They aren't going to reveal anything you don't already know, but they will teach you some interesting quirks about how you work, process, and interact with the world. By studying this kind of thing and processing it offline – thinking purposefully, journaling, discussing with a significant other – it helps us understand why we do and feel the things we do and feel. Over time we get better and better at knowing and predicting how we'll respond in certain situations, and lean into them or avoid as necessary."

Nick mirrors Kevin Kruse in mentioning the personality profile tests like Myers-Briggs and Disc.

"You are independent and confident in your abilities," I said to Nick. "What are your thoughts on the following quote from Muhammed Ali: 'It's hard to be humble when you're as great as I am.' Do you take that quote to be ego, or do you think that since Ali knew he really was that good, he was genuinely stating the fact that it's hard for someone at his level to be humble?"

"No idea," Nick said. "I'll let you know when I get to that level. But seriously, if he's the ONLY ONE at that level, literally everyone else on the planet cannot understand what it's like to be him, so how can we possibly even consider anything else but that he's an egotistical ass for saying it, right? Maybe if you lined up MJ, Michael Phelps, Ali, and a few other greats, and they all agreed that we mortals have no idea what it's like to be as great as them, I'd buy into the quote a bit more.

"But then the relationally conscious side of me would wonder why it was so important for them to need us to know that. I hope I'll always err on the side of humility. At least when a humble person fails, no one's surprised or upset by it. But when a braggart fails, it's open season."

Nick Thacker is amazing, isn't he? He's the perfect mix of humility and confidence, the Mountaintop Mindset and authentic leadership at its finest. And you're going to love who we hear from next.

Chapter 13: Be Yourself

"Be yourself. Everyone else is already taken."
– Michael Benner

Be Yourself

As I was interviewing various experts for this book, I thought about different people I could contact. One person who came to mind is billionaire entrepreneur Mark Cuban, author and successful star of the hit TV show Shark Tank. In watching him, I found him to be very real, and he was someone I wanted to connect with further.

I decided to send him an email. In the email, I told him I wanted to feature him in my next book, and then I asked him, "What is the secret to being authentic in a world that is trying to get us to be like everyone else?"

He responded with two powerful words: *Be yourself.*

Mark doesn't wear a mask – he's fully himself with the people he interacts with, and this is a big reason why his success is genuine. There are a few powerful aspects to consider behind this response from Mark Cuban.

First, it shows that most of our obstacles are internal, not external. I assumed Mark was too busy to respond to me, but I decided to take the risk and email him anyways. What if I never emailed him, out of doubt or fear of rejection? Then I never would have initiated the possibility of receiving a response. The universe rewards action, and the profit in life is for the person who puts themselves out there. The reality is that Mark did have time to respond, but if I shortchanged myself through self-sabotage, then I never would have opened myself up to that possibility.

Second, it's not about what you know, it's what you apply in your life that counts. Knowledge isn't the key to success. *Applied knowledge* is the key to success. How many people know they should be themselves, *but don't do it in reality*? What I love about Mark's succinct and useful answer is that it's a great daily reminder and affirmation. Remember how we were talking earlier about carrying an affirmation on a notecard with you in your wallet or purse throughout the day? This is a perfect example. Print this "be yourself" mantra out. Even frame it if you have to. Make sure to actually apply it in your life, and you will become an authentic leader like Mark Cuban. Being yourself is the key to authentic leadership and prosperity:

- Be yourself in a job interview.
- Be yourself on a date.
- Be yourself when meeting someone new.
- Be yourself with your friends.
- Be yourself with your family.
- Be yourself in all your work and non-work relationships.
- Be yourself while you're kicking back and having fun.
- Be yourself during serious and difficult times.
- Be yourself until it becomes a habit and your default way of being.
- Be yourself when [fill in the blank].

I find this mantra from Mark Cuban to "be yourself" is the perfect reminder before an event of importance (or any event, for that matter). I use it as a reminder before I speak, as well as other events like important meetings, live YouTube discussions, radio show interviews, and things of that sort. Whenever I'm feeling any sort of doubt coming on, I remind myself to "be myself," and it immediately calms my nerves. When you are fully yourself, you never need to worry if someone likes you or not because it doesn't matter – the right people will come into your life, and you will reach the people you are meant to reach.

Stand for Something and Become Iconic

Given Mark Cuban's extraordinarily high level of authentic success, many consider him to be an icon. That's what makes this the perfect time to pull in the example of another quintessential authentic leader, Senator Chris Murphy.

I first met Senator Chris Murphy at the 2016 Jordan Porco Foundation annual gala and conference, and we had a chance to talk face-to-face. He immediately struck me as genuine, and when I approached him, he took the time to chat with me for a while. Senator Murphy is iconic because he stands for what he believes in. In 2016, Senator Murphy spoke in an incredible 15-hour filibuster intended to force the Senate to take up the issue of guns. Gun violence prevention is an extremely sensitive topic, but Senator Murphy is not afraid to stand up for what he believes in. This caused him to become iconic.

For the record, the purpose of mentioning this has nothing to do with getting you to take a particular stance on gun violence prevention. (Note that I did not comment on Senator Murphy's exact stance, I simply mentioned the issue that was at hand; for more information, Google "Senator Chris Murphy filibuster" and read the *Rolling Stone* article). The purpose of mentioning this is to take a step back and look at the primary element in Senator

Murphy's success: authenticity and being fully himself. Senator Murphy *cares,* and his actions show it.

You need to strike a balance between being kind and respectful, while also asserting yourself and standing up for yourself. I mentioned earlier in this book the importance of respecting others. I also mentioned earlier in this book the importance of taking off your mask and being real with others. These two things do not contradict each other. *Both* can happen at the same time. Senator Murphy is the perfect example: He was fully respectful of others, but also stood up for what he believed in by making a stand. His authenticity shone through, and he's making a big difference in our world.

What do you stand for? What do you believe in? What are you here to share with the world? Even when you are fully yourself, some people won't like you for reasons beyond your control. Don't worry about it; recall Winston Churchill's famous quote: "You have enemies? Good. That means you've stood up for something sometime in your life."

"Thank you for your service to the world as a speaker," Senator Murphy said to me.

"My pleasure," I said. "And thank you for everything you do. You're a true leader."

Senator Murphy is humble and down-to-earth – he took the time to thank me, and he didn't have to do that. He's a great leader to learn from.

The Magic Ingredient

I listen to a lot of material from Brian Tracy, one of the greatest authors and speakers in human history. He said something that is one of the most powerful statements I've ever heard: "You don't need to be anyone other than yourself in order to be successful. All you need to do is to be *more* of yourself, more of what you already are."

I've connected with Brian and his team many times, including letting him know about this book you're now reading, and Brian endorsed my previous book, *Reach Your Mountaintop*.

Your success, your authenticity, and your genuine nature is already at the core and truth of your being. You simply need to tap into it and access it! You are already a leader. You are already prosperous. That reality is already there. If you aren't already experiencing these things in reality, it's nothing to beat yourself up over – it simply means you haven't tapped into that part of yourself yet.

We've all been off-course at times. We've all made mistakes. But when you let this epic realization fully sink into your psyche and soul – that you already are what you seek – you'll stop striving to be someone you're not, instead embracing the truth of who you are.

There is philosophical depth behind Brian's statement, but the goal is to think of it as a practical idea you can apply in your life. Here are some quick ideas to get your creative juices flowing:

- You're already a great writer. Now go write that blog post or start that book you've been meaning to write.
- You're already a great storyteller. Now go record that video you've been meaning to record on your smartphone and publish it to YouTube.
- After following the advice of the other experts in this book, you now know what your true values are. Now go live and adhere to them.

The difference between where you are and where you want to be isn't worthiness. You're already worthy. The difference is action. Once you get going, taking action is a lot easier than you may have initially thought. That's the practicality in what Brian said. *You're already there – you just need to express what's inside you.* Of course, you can always get better and improve, but the point is that your wisdom and truth is already at the core of your own soul.

My friend John Lee Dumas, a massively successful podcaster and entrepreneur, mirrors the wisdom of Brian Tracy and the core message of this book.

"When you're just starting out," John said, "it's okay to model yourself after other people. But when you get going, and really find your voice, the key is to be yourself. When I started to throw my true self into my efforts, I really started to succeed. Embracing who you are is the key."

Tapping into the power of authentic leadership and activating your prosperity starts and ends with being yourself, fully embracing all aspects of your true nature. You are lovable and amazing; you are destined for ultimate success.

Keep Going, No Matter What Other People Say

Before we end our time together, there's input from one more expert I'd like to share with you: Senator Paul Formica. I first met Senator Formica at a Rotary gala event in Niantic, Connecticut. A mutual friend introduced us, and we had a chance to connect during the event. We also had an in-depth heart-to-heart conversation on the phone several weeks after meeting.

Before I tell you what he told me, let me say that Senator Formica is an incredibly genuine and smart man. It's *essential* to surround yourself with supportive, encouraging, and inspirational people like Senator Formica.

"What is the secret to your success?" I asked Senator Formica. "How did you get to where you are?"

"I didn't listen to other people when they told me what I could and couldn't do," Senator Formica said. "I didn't let other people stop me."

I included this near the very end of the book because you can apply *every one* of the tips in this book and yet there may still be people out there who will tell you that you won't be able to achieve true prosperity. Be respectful, but don't listen to them. Prosperity is your birthright, and it's yours for the taking. Don't let people take the wind out of your sails. While you are changing for the better, you'll notice other people who refuse to change. Don't judge them and don't react angrily, but refuse to give away your power.

"That's powerful," I said. "What is the secret to authenticity?"

"Look inward, not outward," Senator Formica said. "Recognize your own weaknesses, strengths, and passions. Then ask yourself, *How can I develop these weaknesses, strengths, and passions?*"

Beware of Both Internal and External Roadblocks

"There will be roadblocks in front of you, placed there by people who don't want you to succeed," Senator Formica said. "You'll face these roadblocks from others in any competitive arena. I also want to point out that I had a fear of success. I sabotaged myself because it felt uncomfortable succeeding."

"I appreciate you sharing this and being so open," I said. "A lot of people struggle with the fear of success. Can you talk about this a little bit more, and how you got past it?"

"The fear of success was largely psychological for me," Senator Formica said. "I felt inadequate and undeserving. What I did is I developed a process of goal-setting where I set goals ten to twenty percent outside of my comfort zone."

"That's excellent," I said. "You set goals that were a challenge, but not impossible to reach. What were some of the challenges you faced growing up?"

"I was the oldest of five boys," Senator Formica said. "When I was ten years old, my dad died in a car accident. His last words to me were *Take care of things for me*. I had a great mom and she did everything she could. At ten years old, I put pressure on myself that I couldn't handle. In my early teens, I started drinking alcohol and abusing other substances. This addiction lasted for many years. When I was twenty-eight years old, I realized I needed to stop these destructive behaviors, or else I'd have a wasted life."

"That's powerful," I said. "You had an enormous amount of pressure at the age of ten, and you did the best you could. When you had a turning point at age twenty-eight, was it a specific event that caused you to change or more of a gradual process over time?"

"It was more of a decline over time," Senator Formica said. "I realized I had to say goodbye to my dad, stop drinking, and hello to a new life. This happened in August of 1981. I found within me the strength to overcome the addiction of alcoholism. I realized you can achieve anything you want to achieve."

"That's incredible you found the inner strength to do that," I said. "Your story is incredible."

"When I went to Alcoholics Anonymous," Senator Formica said, "I felt a weight lifted off of my shoulders. It was a physical feeling of relief."

Whatever you are currently struggling with, you don't have to deal with it alone. Whether it be a small problem, a big problem, or anything in-between, there's always help available for you. *Leaders ask for help when they need it.* It takes a big and courageous person to ask for help.

Change the Narrative in Your Head

"There are a lot of people out there who make progress on their goals," I said, "but still face an enormous amount of resistance from family, friends, coworkers, colleagues, and acquaintances. I know you talked earlier about people placing roadblocks in front of us. I was wondering if you had more thoughts on how to move beyond challenges like those."

"When I was drinking," Senator Formica said, "I was hanging out with friends who were also drinking, people who were comfortable living in the gutter. I had to move away from them. I used to love the famous quote *If it wasn't for bad luck, I wouldn't have no luck at all.* To get out of a tough spot you have to change the narrative in your head. We are what we think. I forgave myself and I said to myself, *I, like anyone else, deserve the best this world has to offer.* Changing the record player in my head was very important."

Senator Formica is saying the famous quote he used to love was not a productive or effective narrative to have playing in his head. When he changed the story he told himself, and realized he was worthy, he was able move forward with his life. Also, we all make mistakes. Forgive yourself for the mistakes you've made in the past. Doing this will free you from the pain of your past, allowing you to step into the triumph of your future.

Senator Formica came from nothing. After he graduated high school, he hopped on a bus heading out of his hometown of Cheshire, Connecticut with forty dollars in his pocket. This man is a true leader and inspiration because he shows his true self to the world.

Moving Beyond an Unexpected Tragedy

"You already talked about a powerful turning point you had," I said, "as well as some of the things you overcame. Other than what you already discussed, when was a time you had to deal with an unexpected setback? I ask because I know authentic leaders like yourself deal with unexpected circumstances all the time."

"I started a business with my wife," Senator Formica said. "We opened up a fish market offering clams, shrimp, chowder, and lots of great food. Now it has turned into a ten-thousand square foot restaurant with catering.

"In 2009, the day after Christmas, my wife unexpectedly passed away. She was a wonderful soul and the backbone of the family. She was my life's partner, the person I shared the little things with, and the woman who gave me four great children. She helped with my business and lots of other things. My kids were devastated, and I was devastated. To be stripped of that raised a lot of doubts. This happened right after I was elected as first selectman, and we had just celebrated my re-election.

"Everything is connected and there is power in love. My wife gave love to others her whole life. After my wife passed away, the community wrapped their arms around us and gave us love in return. My wife grew up in the projects of Norwich and did wonderful things with her life."

Senator Formica's wife was a true gift to this world and touched the lives of others. Let's carry her legacy forward by being loving and kind to others.

"As I'm talking to you on the phone," Senator Formica said, "there's a lot of traffic here on I-91. On the back of the tractor-trailer in front of me, the company's name is Rowe. That was my wife's maiden name: Donna Rowe. There is a spiritual energy and if we tap into that, we'll be guided with our circumstances. There are people watching over us from the other side."

Final Thoughts

It's been a true honor to have you on this journey throughout the book. If you'd like to continue the discussion, feel free to email me at jeff@jeffdspeaks.com. Stay true to yourself no matter what, and you'll be the epitome of an authentic leader. See you at the Mountaintop.

One Last Reminder

We've covered a wealth of information in this book, and I'm confident that you are well on your way to mastering the power of authentic leadership. But that doesn't mean your self-educational efforts have to end here. In fact, the next step in your journey is to read my 2nd book, *Reach Your Mountaintop*. The book you just read is actually a *prequel* to *Reach Your Mountaintop*, so this is the ideal next step in your success journey.

As I mentioned earlier, *Reach Your Mountaintop: 10 Keys to Finding the Hidden Opportunity in Your Setbacks, Flipping What You've Heard on Its Head, and Achieving Legendary Goals* is yours for free when you email my executive assistant, Meg, at meg@jeffdspeaks.com.

For more great free personal development content, please check out my blog at http://jeffdspeaks.com/blog/.

Thank You!

Before you go, the team at Jeff Davis International would like to say thank you for purchasing my book. From the bottom of our hearts, it means a lot.

You could have picked from dozens of books on leadership, but you took a chance and checked out this one.

So, big thanks for buying this book and reading all the way to the end. You are in rare company, as most people never read the books they get to the very end. I'm lucky and blessed to have you as a reader.

Now we'd like to ask for a small favor. Could you please take a minute or two and leave a review for this book on Amazon?

This feedback will help us continue to write the kind of content that helps you get results. And if you loved it, please let us know. It also helps expose this book to other people who could benefit from learning about activating the power of authentic leadership.

More Books by Jeff

- Traveling Triumphs: The Improbable in Budapest and Beyond
- Reach Your Mountaintop: 10 Keys to Finding the Hidden Opportunity in Your Setbacks, Flipping What You've Heard on Its Head, and Achieving Legendary Goals

Book Jeff to Speak and Additional Information

Speaker Jeff Davis is an internationally-renowned professional keynote speaker and bestselling author. He speaks to schools, nonprofits, businesses, conferences, associations, leadership development groups, and all sorts of organizations. His expertise is in helping people, especially business professionals and leaders, to activate the power of authentic leadership. He shares practical strategies on how to deal with adversity, overcome bullying, create top-notch teams, elevate your company to the next level, and master your leadership strategy and implementation. His keynote speech and workshop breakout sessions on authentic leadership have been praised by CEOs around the world, and Jeff is one of the world's leading authorities on authentic leadership. His Twitter handle is jeffdavis027, and his Instagram handle is jld016. You can also find him on Facebook via Facebook.com/authorjeffdavis, on Pinterest via @authorjeffdavis, on LinkedIn via LinkedIn.com/in/speakerjeffdavis, and on Google+ as +JeffreyDavisMountaintop27. To subscribe to his YouTube channel, type "Speaker Jeff Davis" into the YouTube search bar or go to Youtube.com/user/27JeffDavis.

If you know someone who would benefit from this book, please refer them to this content. If you know of an audience who would benefit from Jeff's message, please let Jeff's team know.

To book Jeff as a keynote speaker for your next event, please visit jeffdspeaks.com or contact Jeff's executive assistant, Meg, at meg@jeffdspeaks.com.

If you would like to reach out to Jeff directly via a question, comment, or general thought, his email is jeff@jeffdspeaks.com or davisjeffrey222@gmail.com.

Experts Featured in This Book

The people listed below are people I *featured* in this book (the list does not include other authors and luminaries I quoted at chapter beginnings, whom I did not feature at greater length). Please go to their website for more information on how to get in touch with them. If an expert is featured in more than one chapter, they are listed multiple times. If you have any additional questions for these awesome and revolutionary thought leaders, please reach out to them.

Chapter 1

Jeff Davis
jeffdspeaks.com

Chapter 2

Evan Carmichael
evancarmichael.com

Chapter 3

Jared Kleinert
jaredkleinert.com

Chapter 4

Jeff Goins
goinswriter.com

Neale Donald Walsch
nealedonaldwalsch.com

Chapter 5

Pete Kohlasch
yourperspektive.com

Chapter 6

Chris Guillebeau
chrisguillebeau.com

Kinja Dixon
kinjadixon.com

Heather Hansen O'Neill
fireinfive.com

Chapter 7

Suzanne Duret
suzanneduret.com

Chapter 8

Evan Carmichael
evancarmichael.com

Chapter 9

Steve Scott
developgoodhabits.com

Chapter 10

Rick Cleri
He can be found on LinkedIn

Kevin Laylor
He can be found on Facebook

Ashir Nelson
ashirnelson.com

Chapter 11

Kevin Kruse
kevinkruse.com

Chapter 12

Nick Thacker
nickthacker.com

Chapter 13

Mark Cuban
blogmaverick.com

Senator Chris Murphy
murphy.senate.gov

Brian Tracy
briantracy.com

John Lee Dumas
eofire.com

Senator Paul Formica
senatorformica.com

Lightning Source UK Ltd.
Milton Keynes UK
UKOW04f0616201117
313023UK00001B/362/P